*To the searchers for truth
found in the wisdom of the heart.*

ALSO BY
DR WINFRIED SEDHOFF

A Balance of Self: A new Approach to Self Understanding, Lasting Happiness and Self-Truth

The Fall and Rise of Women: How Women Can Change the World

The Friendship Key to Lasting Peace, United Communities, Strong Relationships, Equality, and a Better Job!

Taming Fear in the Age of Covid

REALISING THE ALL (GOD?)

WINFRIED SEDHOFF

REALISING THE ALL (GOD?)

JOURNEYING INTO
FEELINGS AND **BEYOND**

© 2024 Winfried Sedhoff

All rights reserved. No part of this publication may be reproduced, stored in a retrieval system or transmitted in any form or by any means, electronic, mechanical, photocopying, recording or otherwise, without the prior written permission of the copyright holder.

Paperback ISBN 978-1-7636419-0-7
Ebook ISBN 978-1-7636419-1-4

Published by Senraan Publishing
Cover design and typesetting by G Sharp Design, LLC

First edition 2024

Disclaimer:
The medical and therapeutic descriptions in this book are written as general suggestions and should not be considered a substitute for treatment recommendations by qualified practitioners.

CONTENTS

Preface xi

Chapter 1 Early Struggles 1

Chapter 2 The Impossible Choice 13

Chapter 3 Climbing the Inner Mountain 25

Chapter 4 The World Kept Turning 39

Chapter 5 Country. A New Language. A Broken Heart 51

Chapter 6 The Balance of Self Model – Humanity's Heart Revealed? 65

Chapter 7 Women Power – A Cure We Need? 83

Chapter 8 Desires That Broke the World 95

Chapter 9 Mastering Fear and Communicating with Feelings 115

Chapter 10 Feelings – Wisdom, Grounding and Self-Discovery 127

Chapter 11 Love's Secrets Laid Bare 157

Chapter 12 Could The All Be God? 185

Chapter 13 Could Understanding Feelings Be Our Great Future Hope? 197

Chapter 14 Feelings, Hope And Beyond 209

About the Author 217

Acknowledgements 219

PREFACE

It was as if an explosion of joyous light had entered my being and transcended the infinite. Mind and heart were indistinguishable and irrelevant; connectedness had no boundaries; the differences of form, feeling, light, colour, touch – of perception – were but an illusion that restricted the completeness of the brilliance. An ecstasy so immense it was beyond description, transcending time and conscious understanding, had perfused my being.

Finally, after three months of voluntary isolation and pushing my mind beyond limits I never knew existed, of experiencing extremes of terror and sorrow deeper than the darkest abyss, it seemed I had finally achieved what I had set out to do. Hour upon solitary hour of forced mental effort, at times so intense my body felt extremely cold and hot simultaneously, had left me drenched in beads of sweat. I was barely in my mid-twenties and had sacrificed a promising medical specialist career for this, and it seemed the sacrifice was not in vain. Here was joy beyond joy, total embrace, passionate, beyond universal welcome.

But something wasn't right.

Instinctively, I knew there was further to go. It was as though I felt I had reached the top of a mountain but then wondered if this wasn't the peak after all. So I searched and explored, probing deeper, being drawn to a new approach. Then I realised it, subtle beyond measure, peaceful beyond imagining, more practical and insightful than could be naturally contemplated. The light wasn't the ultimate; there was far more.

The transcendent experience – for want of a better description – had a sense of truth about it that is even harder to describe or explain. However, it was also comforting to recognise that what I experienced was beyond anything I might have imagined. This meant what I noticed and realised was less likely to be a creation of my mind constructing what it wanted or needed to believe or know, if my rational mind later had any doubts about the experience's validity.

Some might say I touched God in these moments. But if it was God I was sensing embracing me, it was not the God I had been raised to believe in. Initially, I dismissed this idea of it being God out of hand. However, later, I would reconsider and become more open to the possibility that it was God in a purer sense, uncorrupted by man's desires, fears and distorted interpretations. In chapter 12 we will discuss whether this experience could have been a purer form of realisation of God in more detail. Some might consider what I experienced was spiritual enlightenment, commonly described in Buddhism and other religious texts. From my perspective, it wasn't enlightenment at all – it just was. Recently, I have reconsidered the experience in a new light and recognised many commonalities to suggest an enlightening experience of sorts. To avoid all the myths surrounding enlightenment, I prefer to call what I accessed a transcendent universal experience.

Whatever my new experience was, it left me with a critical choice.

In an instant, I realised I could either continue to explore and gain more understanding across worlds and beyond that I felt were within my reach. Or I could use this experience to help create some inkling of the harmony I was privy to.

Should I preach about this transcendent experience from the rooftops? 'Look what I found!' I could see no point; I had to go to vast extremes to get to where I was, and it would be next to impossible for others to take the same path. So, I chose a different approach – or it chose me.

I intuitively felt driven to try and figure out what was going wrong with the imbalance and unnecessary traumas of this world, especially with its people. My approach? An image came to mind: I would study the problem from the inside by living a relatively regular life – if possible – and see if I could find a way to get back to a state that approximated the level of connection and transcendence I had just felt. If I could do it while still struggling with life's pains, uncertainties and stresses, it could offer insights and give others a practical way to connect with The All, what others might call The Source, The One that *is* everything. It could also give me insight into where the problem might be and what options we might have to try to fix it.

It was an ambitious goal, yet it seemed neither ambitious nor unachievable at the time – it was what I naturally felt I should do.

But what of the reward? What was my pay-off, you ask?

I didn't see any pay-off; there was no heavenly reward at the end, only a more profound sense of harmony, peace and contentment resonating within me. But the task called me – a better-balanced world with much less suffering was more than reward enough.

Now, after more than three decades, I have come full circle. I may have finally realised some of the critical insights and possibilities I was searching for. Perhaps, I have recently learned, the answer I had been probing for is to be found in feelings. But not feelings in the sense of emotions such as happiness, sadness and frustration, but rather something far more subtle yet revealing. What if we could learn to truly understand feelings, use them as a tool and speak their language to transform our lives? More than that, what if feelings and embracing them could get us closer to realising The All – a purer realisation of God, if you prefer?

As we are about to see, feelings can offer us an honest glimpse into our humanity in a profound, meaningful and practical way. They can teach us how to find inner peace and contentment, relieve us of dominating and destructive fears, and take away deep, persistent, emotional pains. They can help revive us and embrace a deeper peaceful, harmonious nature within us, reflected in realising The All.

On a more practical level, learning how to use and understand feelings can even help us uncover some of the mysteries of romantic love, the vaguely expressed nebulous experience touched upon by the eloquent writings of great poets. Imagine knowing what love needs from you to be truly satisfied. Suddenly, we don't have to probe blindly to get our relationships to work; we can look within the feelings that define them, understand them and choose to make our romantic relationships more sustainable, stable and satisfying from the start. Fulfilling relationships becomes our choice.

To my surprise, in the last few years, I have noticed that if we begin to connect with feelings and learn to communicate with them honestly – and we will look at how to do this as we progress through this book – we are automatically also offered a way to directly connect with nature, in similar practical and profound ways indigenous cultures have done before us. Once we emotionally connect with the natural world, we find ourselves just a few short steps from connecting with The All directly. More about that soon.

It may seem simple, but what if the answers and wisdom we all seek in our hearts are waiting to be discovered – there all along?

Feelings, as we shall see, can be infinite in variation and offer endless possibilities. Still, to understand them, we need context and ways to ground us and give us confidence in our discoveries. To learn about feelings, we need a stepwise approach or a framework to build upon. These are offered in chapter 10.

To help add context and practical understanding of feelings, I would like to share some of my experiences that led me to realise The All and events after connecting with it. For instance, I learned the essential value of a sense of genuine self and why we should all look to grow and maintain it. Years after the transcendent experience, I would return to understanding the critical value of a strong sense of honest self, not having fully appreciated its importance till that time.

There were other vital lessons and insights I needed to learn too. Many I would return to and refine later to help others. Some examples include how to conquer our worst fears – how to resolve them, not just calm them down. How to understand, overcome and prevent depression. A hint – a chemical imbalance in the brain does not cause depression. It's about a critical need for connection – too many of us feel lonely. And perhaps some fundamental reasons why women are often treated poorly in our societies, why so much greed currently divides us, and what we might be able to do to alleviate this. Over time, I refined my approach to assisting clients with their struggles, and began to share my insights by writing several self-help texts based on these practical understandings, eventually culminating in this book.

Connecting with The All, I soon realised, wasn't the ultimate; it was barely the beginning.

What could make me want to connect with The All in the first place?

Ultimately, it was as if I had little choice – life compelled me. Events across time, long before I was born, sent me in the dangerous direction of severe depression and I completely lost my sense of self. Once at the limit, I had to choose, see if I could find what others said was impossible, die or die trying – the circumstances had become that intolerable.

It was these circumstances that led to the crisis that helped ensure I would succeed; even if I had no inclination, the troubles I experienced at the time would have a profound benefit later. My salvation would be a journey into the heart to learn how to discover its deepest secrets.

CHAPTER 1

EARLY STRUGGLES

One of the critical factors that led me on the challenging life journey of discontent I have led was that I felt different and unaccepted from a very young age.

It wasn't my colour or religion; it was my race. I was a Nazi. What else could I be? I was German, and all Germans were – apparently – Nazis. I had no idea what a Nazi was; how could I? I was five years old. I had no idea that less than twenty-five years earlier the country where I was born had been at war with the country I had moved to. I had no clue about the lives lost and the tragedy; who tries to explain these things to a five-year-old? What I did know was I was being made fun of – teased by the other children. I learned from a young age how to fight. The teasing may have temporarily stopped, but being excluded didn't.

I remember coming home from primary school one day crying, telling my mother nobody loved me. Of course, she consoled me as best she could – as mothers are wont to do – but she couldn't erase the fact that I was only invited to one birthday party, and that was because my mother worked with the other child's father.

It wasn't all bad; towards the end of primary school, I made a few friends, and we all played a variation of handball together. It was a catching game we called 'butts'. We had to throw the ball against a wall above a line less than half a metre from the ground. The ball had to land on the opposing side of the court and past another line at least one-and-a-half metres from the wall. If the ball bounced twice, then the person closest was out. It was a lot like squash but without racquets and walls all around you. I may not have been anyone's first choice in their team, but I could catch and throw well. I even played in school soccer and cricket teams. I was partially accepted because I was useful but never made close friends.

That wasn't entirely true – I made a close friend once, a kid who kept getting picked on late in primary school. I became his protector. Looking back, I didn't always treat him well either; I became more of a leader than an equal. I helped him improve his grades – I was better at maths – then he left for the USA, and I was back where I started.

Do I remember anything about Germany before we arrived in Australia? Unfortunately, no. I was barely eighteen months old when we migrated. I was born at home, the youngest of two – my sister was over a year older. The picture of the house where we lived revealed a modest, red-brick two-storey in a contemporary design, seemingly newly built. The grey skies and the attire we wore lined up in front made the place seem cold and stark.

My parents met at the local agricultural machinery company – CLAAS – where they worked in Harsewinkel. My mother was in accounts. My father, with a background in mechanics, was a travelling trouble-shooter and salesperson for the company, and his job took him around the world. It was the era of Sean Connery's James Bond,

Ray-Ban Wayfarers, slim suits and even slimmer ties. I remember a dashing picture of him in this classic '60s ensemble with a dark hat to match. He was a slim, good-looking chap. He was inspired to move to Australia while flying over the Sydney Harbour Bridge, peering from a small rectangular window of an old DC-3, the type of two-engine plane used to transport cargo during the war. You still see the occasional old gooney birds around, maybe at air shows, though they are rare. They have been popular with parachuters since they can carry quite a few.

We arrived in Australia in the mid to late '60s and settled in Albury, a small rural city of 30,000 people. It had a CLAAS servicing and sales centre called Alfarm.

It shouldn't have come as a surprise that I didn't fit in and felt like an outcast. There are too many factors to go into here, but I was fighting the odds from the start. Later I would learn how children become a reflection of their parents' prejudices, insecurities, fears and traumas. Much later, I would realise that Western society is mostly not built upon loving welcome so much as divisive competition. It's hard to feel accepted in a society that, by its nature, sees you as a threat to their way of life and standard of living. It is hard when you are a child, however, to not blame yourself for not fitting in – there must be something wrong with me; it has to be my fault. A child has no idea of the more significant circumstances at play that make them feel so different, alone and vulnerable.

My first year of high school was decent. I could still play with some of the guys I hung out with in primary school during lunch breaks and recess. I topped my class academically that year and was moved to the highest academic class the following year – from class 7B to 8A. But, after that, things were quick to deteriorate.

Looking back, I can see the parents' strong expectations of the kids around me to be the best. One chap felt he had to become Prime Minister, and was convinced he could do it. Another was to be a lawyer; he was already top of our year. Most of these boys had ambitions to become a highly paid professional of some type. I initially thought I wanted to be a pilot. Unfortunately, my eyes deteriorated and I needed to wear glasses, so being a scientist started to look good. I could feel the angst when I started getting better marks than some of the ambitious kids around me. Then, one morning, it came to a head.

I was desperately bounding up the stairs, two steps at a time, sometimes three, racing to the safety of the library on the second floor. Most of my so-called friends were chasing me, wanting to bash me. But I didn't harm any of them.

We had been playing cricket in our usual place beside an old flat-roofed, metal-clad, angular gymnasium. A skirmish erupted with some guys from some other classes academically lower than us. It was push and shove. I started to push a chap back, and soon all my apparent friends came over to watch me get belted up – they were egging on the other boy. I couldn't believe it.

It was inevitable.

Throughout high school, up to that point, I had presented some ideas the guys around me disagreed with. One idea that didn't go down too well was about not fighting – I had decided to be a pacifist. I had been fighting so long and felt so alone that when I almost made a younger guy pass out in a fight in late primary school, I had vowed I wouldn't fight again – I finally realised how easy it was to kill someone. Others provoked me many times after the vow became public. Still, I walked away, usually just hanging close to teachers on yard patrol. My idea of trying not to fight was unpopular among the other boys.

I had other beliefs and ideas they didn't like either. It was a time when the fascinating concept of UFOs and the possibility that science and our way of life might not be the ultimate drew my attention. Could there be civilisations and science that were better? I read many books on the subject. First-hand pilot accounts especially interested me; they seemed more believable. I was particularly fascinated with the Bermuda Triangle disappearances. What was science missing? Perhaps the teachers didn't know it all? I began regularly questioning everything. The chaps I hung out with were quick to protect the conservative line of their parents. I learned to be careful about who I spoke to about my developing interests.

It had become evident that I was different from the guys around me and, hence, a threat. Our views were no longer aligned. I was competition. At the same time, I was challenging their way of seeing themselves and the world. It was a volatile radioactive combination bound to reach critical mass.

As the crowd gathered around us, shouting 'fight, fight, fight', I pushed away and past them. Then they started chasing me, calling me horrid names and shouting about how I would get what I deserved, or words to that effect. There were no teachers nearby. I had to run – fast.

The librarian was a lovely lady who kept a tight ship, with no noise or disturbances on her watch. When I scrambled inside the library and slowed down to make it seem okay, she quickly saw the chaps behind me, wanting to get me outside. Thankfully, as they entered, she told them to leave. I was allowed to stay; she'd seen me up here plenty of times.

I felt extremely lonely at school after that. And I was scared. For weeks I had to be the first to leave classes, keep near teachers and spend as much time in the safe confines of the library as I could. Eventually, I thought the guys had lost interest and stopped actively chasing me. The abuse, however, didn't stop but spread. I couldn't walk through the schoolyard for a time without someone calling me names.

I was ostracised.

Why didn't I get help from home?

My father did help once, when one of my teachers in year 7 called me names. I mentioned it to him ahead of the parent–teacher night. He told the chap if he referred to me by my real name I might do better. I did appreciate that. Over time, I learned many Germanic traits from my father that held me in good stead on my internal journey much later, such as always looking for a better way, and if you are going to do it, then do it right and persist.

I never approached my mother about my troubles; she was mainly occupied with trying not to upset my father – typical, I would later find, for women of that era. One of the qualities she taught me was to not speak up or fight back. From this I learned to look for the answers within rather than arguing with someone else.

I have to give my parents particular thanks for allowing me the space to ease my way back into the real world after my revelations. I still appreciate them allowing me to stay on the farm without paying rent or expenses for a much-needed six months. None of what I discovered or realised would have happened without my parents' influence and assistance.

I will share more about my experiences on the farm and essential lessons learned there soon. But back to high school for now …

Yes, I felt alone, excluded and the butt of other people's abuse. But, the coup de gras was the reaction of a girl.

I had my eye on her from the beginning of year 8. It was the time of hormones and great internal rumblings. There was a slight fear mixed with delight in being near her. Sometimes I would try to find a seat close to her or a place to chance a lasting glimpse. I was entranced. Her interests were elsewhere. She mingled with a more popular group.

It was the time of the school fair, and we were encouraged to create stalls to make money for the school. The girl who drew my attention was in an enclosed booth – one of many palm readers. Was she into the exotic too? Was she interested in forces beyond the mainstream? I garnered the courage to go in. I can't remember if she looked at my face. I paid my money. She touched my hand. I have no idea what she said. Wow.

Now I felt inspired to impress. My slight leaning towards exploring what we now call the spiritual took a significant leap.

By that time, my sister and I had wandered from our Catholic upbringing. Many find great solace in Catholicism, but I experienced its nastier aspects. For example, the guys who tormented me the most were Catholic. Several Catholics around me were most affable on Sundays, yet unfriendly and domineering the rest of the week. Most priests were dogmatic and dictatorial – you couldn't question anything. I was once evicted from the confessional because I disagreed with a priest. Nevertheless, I found more answers and hope in other possibilities – the UFOs previously mentioned were just one such interest.

My sister was also interested in UFOs and other unexplained phenomenon. She introduced me to much of it. She recommended an author from the library. His story resonated immediately. The author's name was Lobsang Rampa. He claimed to be the incarnation of a Tibetan monk. His influence on me was powerful and transformative. It also helped me cope and not end it all. It had gotten to where I was considering not being here daily. Life was too painful.

Lobsang spoke of growing up among a secret and select group of monks with special abilities such as clairvoyance and telepathy. He claimed to have undergone a procedure when he was young that opened his third eye to seeing auras. He claimed he could astral travel worldwide and to many realms and see the past and future. He also said he led a life of great suffering, being treated differently, abused and oppressed. It felt like I'd found a kindred soul in the stories of his considerable suffering. He offered a narrative I found appealing.

Lobsang described great wonders of life before life and life after death, of great love and acceptance. There were tales of reincarnation. We come down here to learn, he said. More advanced people will suffer the most – we are so different from everyone else. But, ultimately, we all suffer on Earth and worlds like it to better ourselves like a furnace that purifies metal. Develop sufficiently in this life, and we never have to return – we find liberation.

I needed to believe. I did. I also had my means to impress the girl who never gave me a sideways look. I would work to develop such occult skills.

Then disaster.

The school social was coming up; it was an annual event. I struck up the courage for days, and one afternoon, while the girl of my attention was waiting for her bus, I asked her out. I didn't hear the explanation after the definitive 'no'. I ran off. I cried that night. My mother asked me what was wrong. I told her I was okay and then cried myself to sleep.

The clincher came some months later, as I stood not too far from her on the bus home. She told me loudly and definitively that she had no interest in me, then told everyone I was gay – a common form of the worst verbal abuse of the time. That night I decided she was out – it was time for us to part ways.

What wasn't out were the new beliefs I held onto. I read all of Lobsang's books. Only many years later would I learn he wasn't who he claimed to be. But, for the time being, his beliefs offered me hope and consolation. Soon they would provide direction.

After my brief and traumatic experience of attraction – and being a bit of a stalker – I made a few friends from a year above me – my sister's year. We shared an interest in model planes, and hanging around them made me feel safe – no one bothered me when I was with them. When some of the guys I was hanging out with started taking an interest in my sister and her friends, it was back to the library.

As the end of high school was fast approaching, I needed to decide what to do with the rest of my life. And, again, the stories of Lobsang played a pivotal role. He believed the problem with humanity was an abnormality in the aura, especially in women – looking back, he was clearly a misogynist who blamed the lousy state of the world on the female sex, especially feminism. He postulated that one day we might develop a machine that could read auras and diagnose illnesses before they took hold.

It was early in year 12 – my final year of high school. My sister had returned for a break from university; she was studying veterinary medicine and seemed to be brilliant at it. She was very academically inclined and often topped her class. She even topped her final year in high school. The discussion at the table turned to what subject I would apply to study at uni. I thought I would study physics. However, this idea wasn't well received by my parents, who told me you couldn't make money from that, and there was certainly no job guarantee.

In that case, I guessed I would study medicine. I had to rely on funding from my parents. I had not the slightest notion that I could work to support myself. I had been brought down so low emotionally, I had learned to do what my mother did: give in to keep the peace. Perhaps I was being fated by the universe to follow in the footsteps of Lobsang and find a way to see and correct the aura. My journey would be to help people, though it never felt like my choice.

I had a few other crushes during high school, but none of them reciprocated. Looking back, I understand how transformative a loving, kind, caring and supportive relationship can be, and how it could have changed my life. If only they had accepted me. If only someone had saved me. It became comforting to learn from Lobsang that celibacy was best – be like a monk – you can achieve more spiritually if you do.

I was sick of the heartbreak; I expected rejection and had resigned myself to growing alone. I wasn't even seventeen. Then a new girl who had just changed schools and didn't know my history took an interest in me.

Even so, the rejections and isolation had done lasting damage. Looking back, I was emotionally incapable of having a relationship, the damage was so severe. So when the new and popular girl bravely shared her affection for me one day, I didn't know what to do. Thankfully, she soon found interest in a guy from another school. When we both studied medicine at the same university, I was glad she mingled with another crowd. She took a year off after the first year. I was pleased to hear she eventually graduated. In my heart, I wished her every happiness.

I graduated high school without an inkling of the emotional struggles I would face at university. To top it off, I almost failed in my final year of medicine. My father warned me before I left for Sydney that, if I failed, I would lose his financial support. Similarly, I would lose his support if I joined a religious cult – fair enough – and if I had a girlfriend. I couldn't have a relationship in high school as he forbade that – getting good marks was all that counted. However, my sister had boyfriends on the sly and didn't get in trouble when my father eventually found out. She was allowed to have relationships, as she was always at the top of her class.

Once I started medicine, the family decided I would move in with her and share a rental unit near her university. In the end, there could have been a better plan.

CHAPTER 2

THE IMPOSSIBLE CHOICE

The train compartment was reminiscent of a '50s crime thriller. The long, narrow corridor had large windows on one side and, on the other, windows and sliding doors revealing facing bench seats. We stored our luggage overhead on metal racks. Six or more souls crammed in alongside my sister and I. The green leather, wide benches weren't exactly lounge-room comfort but would have to suffice for the next ten hours of rattling, shuddering and squeaking into station after station – it was all stops, no express. I loathed rail travel to uni on so many levels.

Coming into Sydney was bleak – the grey industrial centres and backyards of the struggling suburbs we passed through made me cringe. The station was busy, the bitumen pathways irregular, and the roof high, arched and ornate. I went to the bus terminal and squeezed aboard with my brown leatherette suitcase, the one with straps and buckles on the front.

It was so impersonal. Even before the era of mobile devices, no one around you would give you more than a blank-faced, sideways look – no smiling, no talking and no greeting.

My sister and I rented a place on one of Glebe's busiest streets. I often had to plug my fingers in my ears at night, especially when the garbage trucks came by. We lived below street level in an old workers-style cottage, three stories, narrow, abutting other almost identical late 19th-century dwellings. Later, wealthy trendies would scoop up and refurbish this highly valued real estate less than half an hour from the city.

I trundled down the worn granite steps, past a small front yard covered in old bricks rather than lawn or scraggly grass. I noticed the date on the I-shaped beam that supported the walkway to the unit above; it was 1880s and made in Scotland. Dark, damp and foreboding, my room was at the very front.

Though I don't recall having much of a say, let alone a choice, we decided to sleep on foldable foam divans. That way, my sister could turn hers into seating; she lived in the lounge room, the next room down the narrow corridor and part of a larger open space. The desks were second-hand; we painted them to brighten up the old wood. The chair was a simple beige, faux-leather, padded kitchen chair that quickly started to get a blue tinge. I would often study in my blue dressing gown with a white trim. I had just come from a small house on a farm – my parents moved there just before my final year. I was used to peering past curtains and seeing trees, sky or stars. This place was old, gloomy, viewless and oppressive – my heart often sank in it, depressed.

On my first day at uni, I felt inferior and unworthy, terrified I wasn't good enough. I made it into medicine by two marks, which made me one of the dumbest, I was sure. I met a few people, mingled and soon noticed a pecking order. The first question others asked was: 'What school did you go to?' The second: 'What suburb do you live in?' The third: 'What do your parents do?' Groups quickly formed around status, though that was only sometimes the case. Surprisingly, I had a few friends in my first year – it was a group of three, occasionally four.

One chap in the group was confident and more mature; he had transferred from another degree. His younger brother studied medicine in the year ahead, so he thought he'd do it too. There was a girl – yep. Her father was a psychiatrist; they lived in a wealthy North Shore suburb. I thought I was the dumbest among them until the results from the first assignments, tests and exams came in.

Many struggled in that first year of medicine. Teachers in the top private high schools had spoon-fed them all they needed to know. The girl in our small group said she would study in front of the TV and hardly did any homework and still did brilliantly. In contrast, at my school, the teaching was so poor in many subjects I needed to teach myself. In chemistry, for instance, I taught myself from a textbook I could relate to that I had accidentally found in a local bookstore. I taught myself a two-year curriculum in less than six months. In top-level mathematics, the teacher was great, but the course was new, and we didn't have worked-out solutions, only answers. All three students of our class and the teacher would have to go home and work on the solutions. The next day, we shared the most concise and simple solution on the blackboard. In contrast, I found out that all the private schools in Sydney had access to the people who wrote and set the subject – it was all just handed to them.

Many of those spoon-fed were struggling to adapt, and their marks were well under expectations, though some – with brilliant photographic-style memories – always made getting top marks seem simple. However, fearing failing and being cast aside by my family,

I studied hard. Thankfully, my marks in the first year were well above average, and some of my anxieties settled.

Sydney, for me, was a hellhole. A desert of concrete populated with soulless people who wouldn't even acknowledge each other. I needed to get out. So I spent many a day on the weekend in a national park. I'd take the train and walk in ancient bushland, often beside expanses of water. It differed from the country walks and open landscape that I was used to, but it helped make the emptiness more bearable.

Then the movie *The Man from Snowy River* opened in the cinemas — a tale of a young man growing up in the Victorian high country. The landscape, the trees and the sounds were so familiar, it made me even more homesick — this was the country I had become attached to as a very young boy, the country that captured my heart. I played a cassette of the soundtrack to the movie so often that it wore out. I knew my sister was sick of hearing it. The melodies were a thread that pulled my soul back to the country's soothing, welcoming, healing calm.

One week the girl in our group asked the rest of us to join her and her mother at their holiday house at Wentworth Falls in the nearby Blue Mountains. There were great bush walks, she said. It sounded wonderful. At the last minute, the other chap pulled out. I had no romantic interest, so this would just be a walk and hanging out with a mate. The waterfall and bushland were medicine, and I thoroughly enjoyed the weekend.

Life at the unit became less tolerable. There was a pecking order, like at home where my father was on top and I was at the bottom. Things needed to be done a certain way. My sister and I began to disagree, and it seemed I would just have to suck it up. Then I had an inspirational visit home during uni break.

The verandas at the front and back of my parents' farm were made from concrete with bumps and divots and roughly painted brown posts. The simple red-brick veneer three-bedroom house was rustic at best – poorly finished was my guess. I never thought I would consider this simple place as home. Home for me was where we had grown up in suburban East Albury. But compared to Sydney, this house, this country I had walked on almost every weekend for over eighteen months before I left for the big smoke, was far more like home than the hostile hole on that busy transit street could ever be. Late in the afternoon or after dinner, I would walk down the dusty gravel road past the front gate to sit under my favourite tree. Then I would meditate, although I didn't know that was what I was doing back then.

The trees are alive like people and other creatures, Lobsang wrote. I sat with my back against this magnificent old eucalypt, one of a cluster near a creek. I imagined the tree as a person and began to feel what it might be like to be this tree, to feel in my heart its connection to the earth, the air, the other trees and the tiny creatures that scurried around and up and down it. Then it struck me. Who does the tree exist for? No one.

Up until that point, I felt I only existed for everyone else. I was insignificant. Everyone and everything else was more important than me, and I was here to assist them. I couldn't have anything I felt I desired; a sense of service to a higher cause at least gave my life a sense of meaning. The tree taught me differently.

No – I was a being in my own right. I was not here just for everyone else. What I wanted and what I was, was as important as any other living soul. Like the tree, I stood alone yet among others with a valid individuality, just as a tree in a forest is a valid entity among a part of a greater country.

When I returned to Sydney the arguments escalated, but I would not accept being second any longer and doing what someone else thought was best. So I began to stand up for myself.

Within months, my sister and I went our separate ways. I moved to a small rental in Coogee, a beachside suburb within walking distance of my university – finally, I could have a proper bed. My sister decided to make some income by being a live-in vet student taking after-hours calls.

My studies began to slide; the regular discipline I had previously of coming home, rewriting my notes and revising the day was now rare. I started to be late with assignments. My mind was in a fight with itself. I wanted to see if I could astral travel, but I couldn't. I wanted to know if I could see auras better – I only noticed a thin blue veil around others. I wanted to learn more about the astral realms. But in the back of my mind was my father's warning. In medicine, if you fail a subject, you have to repeat the year. Failing one subject would mean being cast adrift and on my own.

The connection with my friends had also deteriorated. One day, the girl in our group confessed how she was angry with a guy she knew because he only wanted her for sex. She said she had refused. That night I had romantic dreams about her. Thoughts and feelings arose that I found unsettling.

'I can't see you anymore,' I told her the next day. By then, the other chap from our group of three was rarely joining in; it was just the two of us. She asked me to explain, and I fumbled a response.

It would affect my marks, I tried to explain. She wouldn't buy it. I felt I had something important to do in life, and I felt destined to be alone to do it. In retrospect, it was Lobsang talking, saying you can't see past the veil of this world into the spiritual if you are socially active or in a relationship. You need time by yourself. I never let my feelings grow enough to cry about the break-up with this young, level-headed, attractive woman, but I never caught up with her again to find out her feelings.

I justified my actions further: I recognised I didn't trust I would finish medicine. Lobsang's beliefs about having to suffer in this world, trying to make a difference and selflessly helping others, were fundamental to me starting medicine. I couldn't abandon these beliefs now, not even for this potential romance. To do so would be to lose myself – a terrifying prospect.

I was alone, and I was suffering.

I had felt depressed for most of high school. The depression intensified during university, but not to the point of being unable to study. I still thought of ending it all but couldn't for two reasons. One, it would devastate my mother. The other, Lobsang said, if you kill yourself, you are more likely to return to this world and to something worse. I managed to make it into the final year. Then, I had a crisis of conscience … and I failed the last subject – paediatrics.

I couldn't imagine spending the rest of my life as a doctor; it had never seemed real. Yet, here I was – if I passed the final subjects, the following year would be an internship in hospitals and becoming a doctor. I didn't feel ready.

The uni called me back from a final elective term in Tonga. For your last term in medicine, you could work in a medical place of your choosing. Like several other students, I decided on Tonga, a local Pacific nation of tropical islands. I had been there less than two weeks when I received the call. They gave me two choices. First, I could return and complete the subject again. If I passed, I would then have to sit an oral – face-to-face – exam on all the topics of the last two years. Or I could stay in Tonga, finish my assigned term there and repeat the year.

Repeating the year wasn't an option – I wouldn't have any financial support. I decided to take the first flight back, repeat the term of paediatrics, and do the exam.

The option to return and be examined on the last two years' work was a godsend. By the time I started my internship, all the information was fresh in my mind. It meant I could learn quickly.

The practical skills I learned growing up helped me during my internship, too, especially the endless hours helping my father on weekends. He would make me think ahead when he was making things, like a twenty-four-foot wooden and fibreglass cabin cruiser. During surgery, I could anticipate where I needed to hold a retractor to get stuff out of the way, what instruments to hold and how to assist the surgeon with instruments or get a better view. Surgery seemed simple to me. Besides, I did very well in anatomy at university. It was a pet subject.

The internship went okay. Hospital work regularly threw me into the deep end, from post-operative patients with no discernible blood pressure to chest pains, heart attacks, blocked bladders and many cardiac arrests. Most specialists seemed to like me, which was a good prerequisite for a specialist training placement the following year.

I wasn't too fussed that I had to work over eighty-plus hours a week. I never went out. I didn't drink. And I didn't buy anything. Any interest shown by a woman – often a nurse – was easy to dismiss; I was too busy.

The following year I was accepted into specialist training as a physician. I thought about surgery; I liked it and had support, but that would mean lots of overtime and being on-call. As a physician,

I could work fewer hours if I chose; there was more flexibility. In addition, it would allow me to follow the Lobsang-inspired spiritual pursuits. I started to notice more interest from women finding me attractive. I had time then; I was working far more reasonable hours, and there were no study pressures.

Over the terms I spent in different hospitals – some in the country, others in the city – I felt a yearning for a close relationship. There was no threat of losing support; I had a job now. Could I do it? For the first time, I honestly considered the idea. But that would mean giving up the reasons for starting medicine in the first place and my ambition to have a solitary life. My heart's indecision was tearing me apart.

I needed to clarify my path. What did I want? If I followed my original plan, it would be to research areas that extended beyond the physical. Now that I knew how medicine worked, I could see medicine didn't need devices to look at the aura. But I had ideas about other esoteric technologies that might work, such as a sonic device that could kill unwanted bugs. It seemed more important that I try research.

I resigned before the end of my first specialist training year. My new path was a massive gamble, but I felt compelled to take it. I spoke to a few people at the university and couldn't find a topic eclectic enough. But now I wasn't working, so I also had long hours to contemplate and think.

Did I want to be a physician? Being a doctor never felt like it was my choice; I was doing it to please others and avoid being cast aside and having to make it on my own. Besides, even as I imagined being a world-leading physician, a leader and at the top of my field – the ultimate in medicine – it gave me no satisfaction. So, if I was the best – assuming I could be – then what?

Did I want to be a researcher? The topics and approaches all seemed so narrow, trivial and unsatisfying.

Did I want a relationship? A part of me yearned for one, but at the same time, I knew I was emotionally incapable of having one.

I finally began to see my beliefs were failing me. Lobsang's views were a lie, and although they helped me cope for many years, they were now hindering me, preventing me from living a satisfying life.

Everything seemed like a lie. My life was a lie. I had no idea who I was.

Yes, I could become a physician – if they would take me back – and try to have a relationship and family, but it would all feel fake. The mere thought made me deeply depressed.

I could research, but that seemed unsatisfying, no matter the topic.

I had fallen into massive personal turmoil. My heart and mind were being torn apart in an intolerable emotional hurricane.

What could I do? It seemed an impossible choice.

I saw three options. I could end it all here and now, and I considered it. I could return to medicine and find my way, trying to have a relationship along the way – knowing it would never feel genuine. Or I could do what my heart was now compelling me to do, to see for myself if there were an inner truth, an unquestionable truth that would allow me to connect to the real me and find true life satisfaction.

Lobsang had claimed enlightenment was to reach a higher astral plane. I knew I couldn't trust him. I couldn't trust anyone. If I were going to find this state of knowing that would help me find a genuine sense of self, it would mean giving up everything I believed and assuming everything I had read or learned wasn't true.

I felt I had no choice. I would find what I needed to see inside myself or die trying. But, even if I failed and died, it would be better than living in constant depression and emotional disconnect.

I stopped looking for research projects and sat on my bed in the same rental unit I moved to when my sister and I went our separate ways and began a journey within that could be my end.

CHAPTER 3

CLIMBING THE INNER MOUNTAIN

Light rain trickled constantly on the window behind the closed white venetians, offering the grey noise of near silence. To the right of the window rested the old painted desk from the flat in Glebe, a switched-off Amiga computer the most prominent item on its otherwise stark surface. The bed, standard double-sized with clean apricot-coloured sheets and an off-white blanket crumpled at the far end, faced the featureless, beige-painted wall opposite, beside the door to the right. There were no decorations, no distractions. A pillow protected my back from the stark coldness of the painted concrete behind me – there was no bed head, just the mattress and base. I crossed my legs for comfort, sitting on another pillow. The room was naturally warm enough not to worry about what to wear. Not knowing what to expect, I closed my eyes and began to push mentally. My mind pushed back.

If you are unfamiliar with the mind, you may not know its noise – it never stops unless you make it. I wanted to peer deep inside myself, past all I could sense, and see how much more I could notice. Instead of quietly noticing, though, waves of images and emotions hit me.

For days I cried, noticing my sadness, how unhappy I had been throughout my life, and how unfair it seemed. I blamed my parents and sister for days, filled with anger and resentment. How could they do this to me? I cried, clenched my fists, and walked around the unit many times, on and off for days, before I returned to sitting and trying to focus. Soon I had a critical insight that helped.

No doubt in my mind my family had played a crucial role in how I felt; so did the kids at school and some teachers, but mostly my family – that was how I saw it. Okay, so I blame my parents and sister, then what? But if I blame them, I have to blame their parents, too – their parents played a significant role in who my parents became. Alright, I'll blame my grandparents. But then I need to blame my grandparents' parents and their parents' parents. Then I'd have to blame the societies that influenced all of them. If I were to lay blame, it would have to be on everyone who came before me. That would be silly and pointless. With these realisations, the anger and resentment settled.

I found the path to ultimate connection with The All was littered with helpful and critical insights; I would come to know them as skills and tools. Along my internal journey, I encountered many obstructions I needed to get past or through. The imagery soon came to mind of me climbing a mountain with paths, cliffs and boulders obstructing my way. As I climbed, I would pick up climbing boots here, a climbing hammer there, some metal spikes, ropes and carabiners – all elements to make the climbing easier, critical tools to use as I went. I hadn't yet realised how much these tools would benefit me and others later, for years and decades to come. I cannot recall all of the insights or skills

I gained; there were so many at times. However, some still clearly come to mind and were the most valuable of all.

The meaning of life

Soon after beginning my internal quest, a question soon entered my mind; it wasn't one I expected. What is the purpose of all this – this life, this existence? In other words, what is the meaning of life? I knew I had to find an answer, or this would be a short internal trip. I held the question in my mind; I tried to let it show me an answer. That didn't work. I tried to force it like pushing through thick honey. That failed too. I kept searching for answers. Nothing that came to mind did the trick. I think this happened for at least several days, perhaps a week. Then I had a moment of inspiration.

What if there was no meaning to life, the universe and everything? What if the question was assuming something existed that didn't? Could it be a question was being created that had no answer and never would? But why would we ask such a question in the first place? Why would our brains ask? Ah ha.

What if our brains were made or structured in such a way to ask the question – and the asking was a result of being human? Then there doesn't have to be an ultimate purpose or meaning to life. But life makes us think or drives us to believe there is meaning as a side effect of being human, of our biology.

That did it. The question of the meaning of life disappeared. If there was a purpose or meaning to life and everything, I could never see it, certainly not as one single, tiny human. But who cared? There may be no purpose or meaning anyway – we just are. I could live with that. I moved on.

Truth – confidence in oneself

I pushed hard to notice all things and force my consciousness into the infinite to see what I could. My focus was so intense I felt a cold heat envelop me. Sweat poured from me like a tap; the sheets and pillows were getting wet. At times, I had glimpses something might be there, and I was on the right track; then, another question obstructed my path and wouldn't leave me. How would I know what I found was true?

It was a great question. How could I know that this journey and everything I was discovering wasn't just something made up in my head – a delusion, or worse, a lie?

This journey and attempt could be a complete waste of time. Even though, instinctually, I knew it wasn't.

There was an irony; I was searching for the ultimate truth, and I wasn't even sure I knew what truth was. It was like fossicking for gold and not knowing what gold is, what it feels and looks like.

As I focused the question within my mind and held it there over hours, perhaps days, I suddenly had another insight. What if there are two truths?

Two truths? But surely there is only the truth, the way it really is?

I soon realised there was a personal truth and a greater truth.

The personal truth told me what I was experiencing was real and valid. It confirmed I am valid. My experiences are unique and different from others, but they are still entirely true – for me. This realisation confirmed the insight I gained under the tree during university break many years ago.

I realised that humans exist in their own right and have unique experiences and feelings. These are all different from other human beings, but similar. The difference is essential to realise, or we lose ourselves and stop connecting with and allowing ourselves to feel connected to our bodies or the world genuinely and to our potential.

My desires, feelings and expressions were invalidated when I was treated as the lowest in the pecking order within the family. A psychologist I met only recently reminded me I grew up under emotional neglect. Unfortunately, she was right; I had not seen it in those terms until that point. We lose our truth when our feelings and desires are invalidated and our personal dreams of fulfilment are robbed or taken away from us.

Yes, I learned, I am valid, and my ideas and insights are too. But I can also recognise they are also ultimately wrong.

Why am I ultimately wrong?

Because I only see a small part of a much bigger picture. My views, opinions and ideas about the world and beyond are only observed from the narrow perspective of one limited human being.

Consider the analogy of a beachball-sized globe of the earth. I place it at the centre of a dark room and shine lights on it, making it easily visible. I then get five people to come in from different directions and draw what they see. Later, we all compare drawings.

One person has drawn what was easily recognisable as India. Another drew Europe. Another, the Pacific Ocean and Islands. One had sketched the Americas, and the other, Asia. Who was right? Who drew an accurate representation of the globe? None of them did, and yet they all did. Each drawing was a correct representation of the experience of each person. And yet none of them saw the whole globe, the truth of what it was.

To see the truth of something – if it even exists – means we need to see as many perspectives – points of view – as possible.

What I learned early on my inner journey was to continue to develop my ideas and insights. These views and realisations were real and valid; if I wanted to get close to seeing what is really there – the ultimate truth – I would need to gather ever more information and modify and refine my beliefs. I would need to keep my mind open to the unexpected and be prepared, if necessary, to discard old views.

Should I keep constantly changing my views to the point of starting over each time? No, that would be a waste. So instead, I would aim to keep building on the experiences and ideas as I went. Because I was searching for the ultimate truth and prepared to adapt, I knew if I was on the wrong path, I would find inconsistencies – things wouldn't add up.

The critical insight, I discovered, was the need to search for a *sense* of truth – what felt true for me – and have confidence in it. Ultimately, so long as I recognised anything I currently believed was just a representation of where I was in that moment in time, it wouldn't matter if I was eventually wrong; I would pick up the error later, anyway. The moment I thought I'd found the truth and stopped searching, believing this was it, was the moment I knew I was almost certainly kidding myself.

For those of you who believe in God, I look at the problem this way – having not discarded the possibility that God may exist at this point in my life. If God is truth, compassion, love and harmony, I will eventually find His presence as long as I continue to search for truth. Yes, I may get distracted along the way and believe things that corrupt my purer inner sense of God, but so long as I continue on my quest for truth with an open heart, if God exists, then I will realise Him.

The aim was still to climb the mountain and avoid being misled into thinking I had reached the summit when I hadn't.

Worst fears

It had been well over a month. Progress was slow. Night blended into day and back into night. I focused inside me for at least eight hours a day, often longer, sometimes much less. I slept a bit longer each night. Within ten days or so, my midday was everyone else's midnight. Within another ten days, I'd be back to regular sunlight hours. I stayed in the unit almost the whole time, except for shopping once every two weeks. I lived off homemade chili con carne, raw cauliflower and cheese – I made big batches of chili in one go. I watched a little TV. My mother called once a week, obviously worried and wondering when I'd return to work; she also expressed my father's anxieties on the matter.

I often felt I was being toyed with, like you tease a kitten with the fluffy ball on the end of a string, pulling it away at the last second and making the kitten jump for it once again. Since I had no sense of time, I didn't worry how long this would take – it could take many months, maybe a year or more. I would do whatever it took, no matter how long or hard. Then I struck the most powerful and difficult barrier of all – fear.

Suddenly, all my worst fears and doubts from my past hit me. Having a Catholic upbringing meant seeing demons with the worst possible intent flash before me. They reminded me I would go to eternal hell for this. No redemption, just eternal damnation. I would lose my soul; I would be erased from existence. 'Is this what you want?' they asked.

Now the journey was getting serious. Now, it wasn't just my life on the line; it was possibly life after death, too. Everything was on the line.

I tried all the other skills I'd mustered so far. I tried to examine the fears from a different point of view. I tried to see if there was another way around them and reconsider my path. I tried to push through, but the fears and images became more powerful and foreboding. What could I do? I couldn't give up.

'Fine,' I told them, 'you want to rip me to shreds and cast me into the hell of damnation, even erase me? Do it.'

I let every fear in all its intensity immerse itself in me without any resistance on my part, curious if I would come out the other end. Then something completely unexpected happened. As I felt the full intensity of all my worst doubts and fears imaginable, I felt them fade. Soon, I could see them closer to what they were: a show, a façade, a creation of the fears and doubts of others reflected in my heart and mind. The fears had no truth or substance; they were less than a mirage. It was as if they were a test placed there to weed out the determined from the uncommitted.

The release was indescribable.

I peered deeper, expanding my mind to sense all that was. I was very close.

Good and evil

Removing the shackles of others' ideas, views, doubts and prejudices greatly relieved me. Seeing past all the sadness and fear allowed my mind to consider things more freely. The path to the summit seemed clear.

Immediately, feelings of connection to everyone began to surface, intense and filled with empathy and goodwill. I could see behind the fears and doubts, the bondages I had just faced, their constraining effect on others, and how we treated each other and ourselves.

I realised, despite my upbringing, we are not evil, not in any absolute sense.

But what is evil, I wondered?

Images came to me of people doing nasty things to others. Then visions of a leopard making a kill. Then a rock as comparison, innate, and yet can still take our life if we are struck by a large one.

Then it came to me. It was like trying to find an answer to the meaning of life. There were ingrained assumptions about the question of what evil is. We assume, for instance, evil exists.

But what if evil is like meaning? Is it a product of our being human?

Then I realised. Of course!

Anything that works against us, to thrive and fulfil us as humans, will be considered bad, and frowned upon or punished. We start with children, teaching them what not to do and potentially punishing them for it to prevent them from doing it again. Finally, I could see we, as humanity, took the simple notion of realising what harms us and soon called it 'evil'.

Is killing others good for us? No. We can expect the killing of others to be considered evil. And yet, a leopard kills to eat; that is not evil. To kill to protect our family is not evil. Killing others is not evil, but we cannot condone it except in exceptional cases, or we all live in continuous fear, and our societies will degrade and fall apart.

Of course, it would be similar with good. What is considered good will be what helps us live safe, satisfying lives as individuals, families and communities.

Considering how ingrained the qualities of humanity are within us, it is hardly surprising that human beings would come up with extreme versions of both good and evil, even though, ultimately, good and evil don't exist. Instead, we react according to our nature and the environment around us.

What we didn't see when we created these extreme versions was how others would misuse and abuse the power of these notions of 'beings of ultimate good' and 'beings of ultimate evil'. The idea of good and evil made us open to nefarious manipulation.

Soon I realised it is easier to empathise and feel for others once we learn that people are neither good nor evil. There are very understandable reasons why they act as they do, and nothing supernatural is involved.

Without good or evil, we have a more welcoming heart.

The All – no expectation

With an open heart, I pushed onwards, trying to sense it all – the truth. Within moments, wonder embraced me. I cannot hope to describe the experience, but I tried to at the beginning. It indeed was as if an explosion of joyous light had entered my being and transcended across the infinite. Heart and mind were indistinguishable and irrelevant; connectedness had no boundaries; the differences of form, feeling, light, colour, touch – of perception – were but an illusion that restricted the completeness of the brilliance. We were more than one; we *were* the one.

I'd done it. Finally, after so many revelations, insights, struggles and obstacles, this was it – my mind felt it had no limits, and here was an embracing, endless joy to welcome.

Then I remembered a lesson from my youth. If there are strong emotions, be wary; strong emotions cloud the truth.

Yes, I had felt strong emotions for others, like the girl I had a crush on in high school. Intense anger and hate clouded my view of others, making me unable to see others' points of view, struggles and plights. Truth, I learned early, wouldn't be found in strong emotion but in calmness, allowing clearer reasonable thought.

I began to doubt. Could this powerful emotive experience be a deception, too? I'd thought I'd made significant breakthroughs before on this internal journey and been wrong. Was I making a similar mistake?

But I wanted to believe this was it. Ah, that was the clue.

If I wanted or needed it in any way to be true, then I could be pretty sure it wasn't what it appeared to be.

So, I put aside the embracing joy and light and probed with my mind to see beyond it.

Soon, I realised that the only way to perceive all things was to have no distortions, emotions or expectations. An image came to mind as if answering my call – nothingness.

Could I be nothing?

Logically, trying to be nothing sounds absurd, but it wasn't such a silly notion in the scheme of what I could now perceive.

I began to see if I could be nothing, making it real, immersing myself beyond darkness – since darkness is not nothing. Deeper

I went, immersing in the nothingness more and more. Then I finally realised I could be nothing, but that would be such a waste.

I existed and could grasp a greater sense of what that meant, some of the vast potential. Everything had come to create me as I am; why not use it?

Looking back, if I'd chosen to be nothing in that moment of inner self-exploration, I have no doubt I would have died.

Then it occurred to me. To perceive nothing and perceive everything was the same thing. For something to exist, some form of change must be noticeable, like the movement of a fly or the fading of the light. So at some fundamental level, to exist, there must be change. But when we perceive all things across all times as one, ultimately, we sense there is no change – it just is.

Without expecting it, noticing and immersing myself in nothingness suddenly gave me awareness and connection with The All.

Here there was no distorting cloud of emotion. On the contrary, as feebly as I might describe it, this was the most subtle of feelings spread beyond eternity, far across existence as we know it, and infinitely beyond.

The realisation I sensed was that I was The All, and The All was me.

This experience was as close as I needed to realise …

This was the mountain peak.

CHAPTER 4

THE WORLD KEPT TURNING

I still paid my rent. I still went shopping. I showered every day and every two to three weeks I would wash my sheets. I had my car serviced and filled it up, though I wasn't driving it much. Cars left from the block of units to go to work in the morning and returned in the evening. It still rained, continuing to fall more than usual for this time of year. I may have connected with The All, but the world still turned. What was different was how I saw and felt about it. I very quickly had to make another critical decision.

By this time, I fully realised I was part of everything and everything was part of me. Answers and insights came almost instantaneously without prejudice, fear or emotional need. What might have taken me weeks in the past to realise now took moments, or so it seemed. All the influences of my life to date, though, hadn't left me. For instance, I still had an enormous curiosity about how everything worked and how it came to be. A realisation that enticed me was that I could see so much, yet so little, simultaneously. Today, the analogy I use is of the old computer games.

When home computers became a thing, the search was for speed and memory. I loved playing games, especially flight simulators – you may recall that I once wanted to be a pilot. With simple graphics, the images in the distance were composed of large, ill-defined pixels or blocks. The detail was reserved for what was right before you to create a sense of realism; the background and everything else was too blurry to make out. It was similar to my state of perception within The All.

I could sense the outlines of anything and everything, but it had no detail. It also had no meaning. I quickly realised I needed to take a point of view and restrict what I was focusing on – like taking the perspective of a human being, for instance – or I couldn't make any sense of it. We take for granted how our minds need context to find meaning.

What do I mean by context and meaning?

There have been several cases of children born blind who, once they became adults, could be cured and able to see. But when the blindfold came off, and the light was visible for the first time, they could neither make sense of the light changes nor give them any meaning. The new stuff they saw was next to useless for them until they created associations – connections to what meant something already. Consider the example of a glass of water. Before they had any shimmering of light to notice, they already associated the glass of water with other senses such as touch, taste and smell. Even without seeing, they knew what the glass and water were for – to hold, drink from and so on. Now they had to add a visual representation to what they already knew was a glass and water. They began to learn to give what they could now see context and meaning. Until then, the lights and colours just were.

What I found in the transcendence of the experience of The All was that, unless we take a point of view, it all has no meaning and isn't relevant.

For a moment, I thought about looking further afield from the perspective of a human being and perhaps as other beings – there were many points of view to choose from – and see what I could discover. But then, I almost instantly decided against it. So instead, I would follow the path I mentioned earlier of returning and trying to better understand the human condition and imbalance.

At the core of the challenge was to see if I could truly understand the heart and mind of a human being – of us existing in this temporary form before we return to being part of The All. I wasn't going to use science since I saw it as too restrictive, sluggish and completely unaware of the influences outside the physical. We will talk more about science as it pertains to exploring feelings and The All later. For now, my method to better understand the human condition would be through questioning, persistence, adapting and searching for a sense of truth.

In other words, I would plunge into the depths of the heart and our inner being and sort out how it worked in some helpful, practical, insightful way rather than use science or other writings as the primary source of information, inspiration or knowledge.

I returned to my sitting. Little did I know the approaches I would soon discover could help overcome and prevent mental illness, offer guidance to others in distress, and help in the pursuit of lasting satisfaction and contentment.

Without realising it at the time, I was also setting a path to understand feelings better and how we might use this insight to get us closer to The All and be able to experience it more completely.

The question that soon entered my mind was, how do I understand the human condition in its rawest and most basic sense? If I was The All, for instance, how might I create a human point of view out of its infinite variation or even from nothingness?

The basics of what it is to be human

I realised even before we develop a human way of noticing or perceiving everything – a human perspective – we need to create a point of view, a place to witness everything from.

What do I mean by creating a point of view? Consider the following example.

When we peer across a valley, we don't see it from all perspectives, from the air, the land, the water or the sky all at once; we see it from one perspective, one point of view. Like we might stand on a rock to see across the vista below, or from a tree or a plane, but The All's perspective is noticing everything across all that is and beyond the infinite – there is no point of view that is meaningful to witness it all from unless we restrict that view in some way – create a point of view.

What restricts our perception when we are capable of noticing so much?

As a person who likes to know specifics, I went back even further to ask how we might create the basics of noticing out of nothing – way before being conscious. I won't bore you with the details; I soon realised that, in its most basic sense, noticing comes down to change and creating associations between the changes. Change is even more fundamental than matter or energy, yet there is no universe without change. Without a universe, there is no point of view. I write about this more in the final chapter of this book.

For the fun of it, I later developed basic physic principles based on these realisations about change that helped me to see the illusion of the physical and how it can be created – that, ultimately, there is only the illusion of time, energy, distance and matter – it isn't at all as it seems. The theories quickly predicted how gravity worked and automatically explained time dilation – a property tested and predicted by Einstein's theory of relativity. The ideas also just happened to suggest the practical possibility of time travel and travel across different temporal states or realms. It seemed one realisation opened the mind to many valuable and useful perspectives. The physics insights reaffirmed for me that we are quite literally all connected.

But the question remained: if you were The All, how might you create a human point of view from its infinity? The human point of view is not just defined as physical but can also be beyond that. So how would we create that restrictive point of view to give us human qualities of seeing, noticing and participating across the realms of the universe? As I posed the question, soon an answer appeared – feelings.

At the core of being human are the experiences we can recognise as feelings. Our feelings determine our human viewpoint – the fundamentals of our humanity. We will discuss how feelings define our humanity in more detail soon. Suffice to say, I could see how feelings were the foundation of our individual being that defined us as humans appearing to be separate from everything else.

Okay, if feelings define us as human in the most basic way, how many feelings do we have? I searched, looking inside myself and into my past experiences to notice how many feelings I could experience. This search looked beyond emotions to include sensations of even the most subtle type. We always feel.

How many feelings could I recognise? Infinite. It was like a flowing cloud of endless sensations, emotions, thoughts and imaginings – like a creek within a river, a sea, an infinite ocean.

Great, how can I comprehend the infinite? Well, I did when connecting with The All, though I didn't find that helpful here. Then an image came to mind of a measuring ruler.

Imagine at one end of a ruler, there is absolute white – the purest white in existence. At the other end of the ruler is total black, so black not even a speck of white exists within it. In the centre of the ruler, there is an equal mix of black and white – grey. As we travel towards the white, the grey becomes lighter until it becomes white. As we journey towards the black, the grey gets darker until it becomes pure black. How many shades of grey have we just created?

Infinite.

Brilliant. Feelings, I realised, could be comprehended. All I needed to do was find the two extremes of the most primitive or basic feeling, and it would explain all the rest.

The whole process of understanding feelings is analogous to understanding colours. How many colours are there? Infinite. Like a rainbow, the colours blend seamlessly from one colour to another. How do we make sense of how many colours there might be? We can create any colour by combining three primary colours: red, blue and yellow. Then we can create an infinite rainbow of colour. It is similar to feelings.

We don't need to work out how many feelings there are to make sense of them; we only need to recognise any primary feelings – like primary colours. Then, blend the primary feelings, and we should be able to recreate any feeling we experience.

But what feeling is the most basic of basics that I always feel is always there?

Do you know?

What feeling within you is ever present? It might be so subtle you barely notice it; at other times, it can be so extreme it overwhelms you with emotion. Do you recognise such a feeling within yourself?

For me, the answer was fear.

Fear is always there. It could be so small to keep us barely awake or so severe it leaves us petrified and soiling ourselves.

If I'd grown up in a society filled with love and compassion, I might have chosen one of those feelings, but I didn't. Instead, sadly, we live in a society dominated by fear that easily overpowers any all-pervading love and compassion laying beneath; fear in some form seems ubiquitous in this life.

But did fear explain everything I felt? On its own, no, it didn't.

Fear, I saw, often tended to make me avoid things that might hurt or harm me – like getting in trouble with my father or not standing too close to a cliff. I would later learn the rest of fear's secrets and how to help others master it, but at this point, I saw fear as a way to avoid and protect.

What was missing in my understanding of feelings was what drove me to do things like eating, drinking or keeping warm. We don't search for water or food out of pure fear. What was missing was what we call desires or motivations.

Desire is key

I want. I need. I feel sad about the loss. I feel joy in hope. But, on the other hand, if you humiliate and reject me, and I am attracted to you, I feel emotional pain. Desire, I now realised, was the key to unlocking my heart and unravelling the mystery of feeling as a human being. Within the heart of desire is what we call instinct.

As creatures, we have instincts, biological drives or imperatives that keep us alive and ensure we reproduce and thrive. If we don't satisfy them, we can quickly perish. We may experience these instincts as desires and motivations, feelings inside us that propel us towards doing things.

When you crave a lover's physical touch, seek a supportive parent's warm embrace or curl up under a warm blanket on a crisp night, these are all examples of us experiencing desire. And it can be magical. Satisfying our desires and the pleasure that goes with them can be divine. But desire comes with a flipside.

Being ostracised and alone, the divorce of our greatest love, losing the ability to provide for our family – these are all examples of desires unrealised, of promises and dreams snuffed out like a candle. To know pleasure is also to know the pain of desires unrealised or taken from us. Desires are a blend of many feelings, including pleasure, promise, hope, emotional pain and regret.

In other words, behind all desires are basic human instincts or needs. These needs, with the feelings of fear, primarily define our humanity. Just as the instincts of a leopard drive the imposing cat to hunt, kill and live a mostly solitary life as an apex predator. Just as the instincts of a dolphin drive it to eat fish, socialise and mate, then carefully raise its young and ride the surf. We are creatures too; we are human creatures, and our instincts, our basic desires, are as unique to us as a species – a people – as those of any other creature are unique to them.

Peer into our hearts, and we find the essence of our humanity – how The All has defined us to be.

What about the human senses of taste, touch, sight, smell and hearing? Where do they fit in?

Our desires and fears shape all the physical sensations we experience. For instance, it tastes good because we need to eat to stay alive. Looking over the edge of a cliff brings a racing heart and sweaty palms as we experience fear warning us of danger. And yes, it will hurt if we severely injure ourselves; the pain is part of our desire to heal.

Had I found the answer? Were we, at our most basic, just a combination of fear and desire?

I searched inside, as always, looking for evidence from experience and observation rather than what I may have read.

It seemed true. As I blended infinite variations of fear with endless variations of desire, cravings, displeasure and joy, I could simulate and recreate all I had ever experienced and felt. More than that, I could predict how others might feel and react as a result.

Human beings, as I had learned earlier, are predictable. At heart, it seemed, we are very basic indeed.

Peering into our hearts and understanding the fundamentals of our humanity was a powerful early lesson. How powerful and valuable it wouldn't become apparent for decades. In fact, it would take years of experience and heartache before I developed a usable model to help us recognise our basic human desires – to give them functional names like discovering primary colours. I would call it The Balance of Self Model and find it invaluable in assisting others to overcome depression. More on this in chapter 6.

I could see that to be human was to embrace desires rather than try to reject or run away from them. To be human is to explore the sensual and integrate it into our lives without guilt. I instinctively knew we could do all this balanced and respectfully. As a result, I began to see we have the potential for a sustainable, balanced life that could be far more about pleasure and contentment than pain and fear.

With this new insight into feelings, I began to question how I had become who I was. I sought to redefine and rebuild myself by seeing all things in new ways based on these unique experiences – to build new foundations of my humanity and ego from scratch if I could. I didn't know if it was even possible. I was struggling to make headway when a great teacher appeared. Her name was Zoe. She was a one-year-old sheepdog whose life was on the line … she was about to be shot.

CHAPTER 5

COUNTRY.
A NEW LANGUAGE.
A BROKEN HEART

The bedhead was a basic wooden frame with an angular light added to one corner, covered by an opaque plastic fascia. It was the familiar single bed of my youth now in the back and smallest bedroom of the farmhouse. Outside my window to the right was the small brick garage converted into a workshop. Past it was a large, covered area for machinery and, beyond that, a large hay shed, often packed at least three-quarters to the roof. As you headed to the roller door of the workshop, on your left was a two-metre by one-metre wired-off section with thick, rectangular wire mesh welded to metal posts. Under its slanted flat metal roof, smooth concrete; in the far corner was a wooden box with an opening and small veranda. This construct was Zoe's house. She went crazy with anticipation. It was time to go to the back paddock to play with some sheep.

Months of meditating and questioning had meant my money was running out – I'd used my savings sparingly, and an excellent tax return helped to keep me going for a while. My mind had many questions about what I felt, how I was thinking and why – how the mind and the world worked. I was finding answers, but then more and more questions or insights consumed me. I felt utterly unable to work and wasn't sure if I would ever return to medicine. Knowing I needed much more meditation time to sort myself out, I attended a Tibetan Buddhist centre in Melbourne. I actually contemplated being a monk.

It was a lovely teaching centre in the heart of an expensive suburb filled with broad, quiet, tree-lined streets. The large flowing branches of the majestic old European trees – I can't recall the type – offered shade and serenity to this calming place. The people seemed nice, but I quickly learned to join such an institution was to follow dogma and texts and not spend days in meditation. The meditations they did there were guided, with no room to explore and take further what I had already learned. Nope, being a monk wasn't going to work. Thankfully, my parents let me stay on the farm until I could work out my next move. I sold, gave away or donated most of what I owned except for my car and clothes. I even sold my old purple high-school bike I used to ride around Sydney. This would be a new start.

When I arrived at the farm, it was almost instantly apparent my routine was out of sync with my parents. I would stay up until 2 am or later, then get up in time for lunch. I know my father wasn't impressed; he would often do the loudest construction or jobs in the workshop next to my window early in the mornings, even though I knew he could do them just as well in the afternoons. On my first day back, Zoe and I introduced ourselves. She was a new working asset. She was full of beans and bright as a spark. Unfortunately, there was talk of her being put down.

Farmers, by and large, are a practical lot. You get rid of it if it doesn't work or earn its keep. Zoe's head was on the chopping block, or, to be more accurate, the nasty end of a gun.

My father knew nothing about sheepdogs; Zoe was his first. She was a German Coolie, a dog about the size of a whippet, lean and slight, like a miniature greyhound, with a lovely long coat of mostly black fur mixed with some white. Imagine a thin and small, black and white Border Collie, and you'd be close. The problem was the local farmers regarded her as a splitter, a poor trait for a sheepdog the local experts said that couldn't be trained out. I knew she was trainable; she was so bright. I wasn't going to let her die. Now I had a regular job.

A splitter meant that instead of the dog running around the sheep to keep them together, she would break them up through the middle. I watched my father try to work with her. Once she saw the sheep, she was off, and no calling or instructions made a difference. She'd run circles around them a few times in enthusiasm and delight, then rush through the middle. When worn out, she'd come back and sit as commanded. My father had been informed she'd been trained, but it was apparent she wasn't. I didn't then realise Zoe would teach me much, including essential human, child and dog psychology. Later, I would learn she was teaching me a new language, too.

One of the more valuable traits that came to the fore after my connection with The All was my empathy had increased. Regarding Zoe, it was as if I could read her thoughts and feelings and anticipate them. At the time, I theorised that our mind builds on small steps – we learn and then build on what we know. It was helping me make sense of my past, and how I came to be in the troubled position I found myself in less than a year ago. I realised we could not learn everything instantly; we learn and get good at one thing and then add to what we just learned – progressive steps. I remember getting in trouble as a kid for not knowing something. But how can you know if no one teaches you the steps, like learning to count before you start addition, subtraction, division and calculus, for example?

It was similar to when I was in The All and the transcendent awareness; everything wasn't available to know and use suddenly. It had to be learned in parts – the whole wasn't practically available. For instance, I suddenly couldn't play the piano even if I could comprehend how.

I instinctively knew what Zoe needed were lots of small training steps. The first lesson Zoe needed to learn was to sit. She was quick to remember that. Then she needed to learn to listen, no matter how excited she became, so she would follow instructions. How would I get her to do that? A long lead.

The long lead I made out of bailing twine and other bits of thin rope attached to a choke chain around her neck. Fortunately, some sheep were in the home paddock just outside the wire fence around the house and its gardens. I made commands for her as I went; I had no idea what to give her as this was the first dog I'd ever trained. I would sit her beside me, and the sheep would approach the fence, grazing. Zoe was raring to go. I'd say something like 'okay', then as she shot off towards them, I'd call out 'STOP'.

I held onto the lead, and once she was at the end of it, she'd have to stop. I'd call her back and give her lots of praise. We did this for several days; she soon got the hint. In no time, she learned to stop on command on her own – she'd started to listen. Again, I'd call her back and give her lots of affection for an excellent job.

At least one to two hours of training per day was our routine. I could see why my father struggled with her; she constantly tested the limits to see what she could get away with – and what would get praise. However, I don't think my father noticed these signs of intelligence; he just expected her to do what he had been told she could – round up sheep. It wasn't until much later I realised Zoe was behaving so much like a young child – testing what they could and shouldn't do, seeking praise, affection and attention.

In no time, I was happy to take her to the back paddock about two kilometres down the gravel road out front you could call our street, then through public land and to paddocks of around three-hundred acres peppered with a few trees and dams. I enjoyed this country, open and flat. Zoe, as ever, was running in circles with excitement before I'd call her onto the back of the motorbike.

The step-by-step approach worked. I called Zoe, and she would come. Then I'd get her to sit beside me, even though I knew she just wanted to chase the four-legged woollies. We started by working the sheep along the fence. I'd call her back to keep them moving – go back and forth to make sure there were no stragglers – then if they broke loose, I'd get her to chase them down, bring them back and then sit by my side. Hour after hour, day after day, in the cold or wet, we played – I could see this was play for her, not work. Soon we could work the sheep away from the fence. Then came the big test, and I knew she had the skills.

We arrived in the paddock with the sheep spread out in the distance. I gave Zoe the command to bring them back; she was off like a shot. In this large paddock, she rounded up the sheep and kept them together as she brought them back. I couldn't help but smile in amusement when I saw her head jump up from behind the mob occasionally to see where I was. I was able to give some hand signals from a distance.

It took months of play. Zoe was no longer a splitter. Zoe became one of the only reliable working sheep dogs in the region. My father couldn't get her to do as much as I could, but she could move sheep along roads, prevent them from breaking free, and drive them into a yard. Her yard skills weren't so excellent; she'd previously been abused. I could tell by how she would cower easily and sometimes be intimidated by sheep who opposed her. I never struck her for doing the wrong thing; I was more focused on praising her for what she did right. Instead of corporal punishment when she did something wrong, I'd use a stern voice. Better still, ignore her. I'd call her back to me, get her to sit and not praise her, then send her out again.

I learned many lessons from Zoe I still remember and use today – for instance, the need for repetition and consistency. If I let her get away with something I didn't want her to do, it could take another twenty times before she'd get it right. I learned early during our sessions that no matter if I was in a good mood or not, the rules – the limits – had to remain the same, or her intelligence would see her try to please me by doing things I didn't want her to do. I learned to hold back my frustrations, and be calm and regular with praise.

Praise became the key. As I thought about it, I realised Zoe would remember the recent events I praised her for. So no point in getting angry with her for something minutes ago; the praise had to be immediate or pretty close – praise what I wanted her to do and ignore what I didn't.

Later, I would realise that is how our brains work too; when we receive praise, the connections it just laid down as part of our experience become reinforced and stabilised for use again next time. In terms of Zoe, this also meant ending the day getting it right. If the last lesson or experience wasn't what I was after, then the next day, she would start on the wrong foot by doing things I didn't want.

It can be similar with sports people. The last shot or actions at the end of practice get laid down in the brain for next time. So if we want to improve at anything, we must end the session by doing what works, so it becomes what we do next time.

In other words, try to always end on a high note, the way we want it to be next time.

Outside of playing with Zoe, I would go for long walks or rides on the motorbike up the back ranges. Other times I'd help my dad with farm work – farms never stop. My mind was often in torment, as reflections of my past traumas and troubles still came forward to bother me. Finally, I realised that, although you might get to perceive beyond yourself in perceiving The All, your past habits, thoughts, triggers and troubles are still inside you. It is like being more aware and having more understanding, but still being in the same old vehicle.

Being on the land – what some term 'country' – was enormously soothing. The experience of connection with The All allowed me to feel nature and listen to her in ways I had never considered or imagined before. My affinity for trees grew more robust, but so too it did for the country itself. Without knowing it, I was learning a new way to understand language. This skill would become invaluable when understanding, using and changing feelings later.

Zoe and country had been talking to me. But not with words. I was only beginning to listen.

The top of the home paddock of just over a hundred acres had a gentle slope up the back, with a well-wooded range behind it. One of my favourite places to sit other than under a tree was on well-worn lichen-covered rocks barely breaking free of the surrounding earth.

Before me was a vista flat for as far as the eye could see, dotted with farms, crops, green acreage and clumps of tree lines. To my left, a small, gently sloping hill still had its natural cover. Later I would learn this is Wiradjuri country – a proud and insightful Indigenous people. I didn't just sit and stare at its calming beauty; I could feel it as if still in connection with The All. I could sense the country as if it could speak to me, not in words, but so much more profoundly.

As I let myself feel the nature of the country before and under me, I tried to feel what it may sense or notice as if it were a person, like we are part of the greater All. I felt without expectation and noticed a subtle sadness. It all felt wrong. The country wasn't being heard but trounced upon with disregard. But what could I do? I asked in my heart. Then an image from my medical training came to mind; of all things, it was a T-helper cell from our immune system.

The T-helper cell is a white cell that helps us fight off cancer and infection. It essentially locates the damaging foreign intruder or locates the cells that have grown outside of their usual place and become cancerous. No, I could not save the world, and it would be arrogant and naïve to believe I might, but I could be a helper cell. One cell of millions, who can make other cells aware of cancerous change afflicting us and the world, and help to focus on the areas that need tending. I do not care where this image arose or why. The most significant strength for me was the connection to country itself. It wasn't just Wiradjuri country; I felt it was as if it was a part of the greater earth, like a tree or mountain or a dog is part of the greater whole.

As I returned to this place many times, I would eventually contemplate the nature of language. Could a dog or land speak to me? Could I learn to listen?

Images of us as human beings before we could speak came to mind, of people communicating without words or many sounds. Can we communicate without verbal language, I wondered? Today we call it sign language but, I quickly realised, that communication can go much deeper than that.

Before we could sign, we could read how other people might behave, how they might react and what they might do. We could predict this just by being with them. All their motions and expressions would have meaning for us. For instance, if they clenched their fist a lot and huffed and puffed, it was probably not a good time to get too close, or they might thump us – today, we would recognise this as anger, frustration or irritation. In time, we could get a feel for what people were about, a sense of them. Today we might call it nonverbal communication – actions and behaviours, often subtle, associated with meaning.

Later, we gave noises meaning too. Soon verbal language was born, but as most people familiar with language would agree, most human communication is still nonverbal. Some might say it is 80% nonverbal; I estimate it is closer to 90% or more.

To be on country, I learned, is to read the country's changes to know its meaning. Then, if we listen, it tells us great stories about itself, which we can use to guide us as a people.

Even Zoe was communicating nonverbally with me. I could read her moods and intentions so well, I knew when she was about to do something wrong before she did it and said, 'Ah, don't think about it!' It was as if she was a small child caught putting her hand in the candy jar knowing she wasn't supposed to. The expression on her face said, 'I wasn't going to do it; really, I wasn't!' Yeah, right. But I knew she wouldn't do it again if I caught her about to do it and stopped her first.

If we listen with all our senses, everything talks to us and tells its story. We listen by connecting to our feelings – how we feel about a place, person or thing. Without words, we can learn and connect with so much, especially in nature.

I sometimes envy the level of language connection indigenous peoples have had with their country. I look forward to once again when we learn to read and communicate with nature and respect her language. But learning the language of country and nature has an even more powerful, profound and potentially more significant positive effect. Listening to nature is less than one step away from listening directly to The All. I learned in my transcendence that nature is a direct expression of The All in its purer physical sense. We are The All, and The All is us. So too, we are nature, we are country, and nature and country are us. What we do to one, we do to ourselves and everything.

It would be decades before I finally realised feelings have a language, too and learning its language connects us to everything almost directly. But first, I needed to experience the heartaches and pains of relationships and life.

By the time my credit card had maxed out, I knew I had to leave the farm; I wasn't going to ask my parents for money, and I could see how eager they were for me to make a living. I found an advertisement in a Sydney newspaper. I applied for a job in a medical practice in the Northern Beaches of Sydney. I drove up there for the interview, and before I knew it, I had the job. It was tough at first. I had no GP experience, only hospital and emergency department work. Thankfully, what I had previously learned all came flooding back. I would figure out much about being a GP through trial and error, asking questions and talking with specialists. I worked part-time. I still needed plenty of time to myself.

I felt lonely within several months to a year – I never thought I would be, but I was. Then, a vibrant young patient of mine invited me to a BBQ to watch the rugby grand final, and while I wasn't into rugby, I went anyway. Afterwards, I started to have visions I could still follow my greater learning and have a partner too – maybe a family?

Within a year, I met someone and we were together for four years. We explored much together physically and otherwise and had some fun – though, like most relationships, we had our ups and down. Only years later would I realise we were never truly close friends; there was so much I couldn't explain to her – a distance grew between us. Once she'd started an emotional affair behind my back, it ended. I cried for days when she told me it was over. But relationships weren't off my radar – yet.

I had a primarily physical relationship with an attractive young salesperson I met through work. It lasted six months. Within a month of me ending it, she came to me and said it was never going to work anyway because she put her career first. It is true her work kept a distance between us, but this relationship also wasn't grounded in a close friendship. So again, there was a barrier between us.

Third time's a charm, they say – well, not in this case, which set me up for the most significant disaster. I started a relationship with a part-time model who enjoyed the party scene but told me she wanted to put it behind her and settle down. She already had a three-year-old son from another relationship, and the father was living in Melbourne. I took her at her word, and over time, increasingly cared for her son, as she spent more and more time out with her friends at clubs. Never before had I known such verbal and psychological abuse. What troubled me was that the abuse got worse if I didn't stand up for myself and argue back. I'd never even been in a heated argument in a relationship before. The relationship continued for twelve months; it should have ended after two.

Why didn't I leave earlier? Many reasons, looking back. One, it was like boiling a frog. You put a live frog in the water in a pot above a fire, and as the water slowly heats up, the frog barely notices the changes – until it is too late. Second, I believed it could get better. I had the arrogance to think I could solve this; it was a psychological problem to which I could apply my insights, and it would be fine. I was wrong.

And besides, I felt for the kid. His mother neglected him, had no home of her own, and was financially struggling.

The severity of the abuse made me doubt everything about myself, including what understandings I had learned. Then, as part of the abusive ex's departing words, she told me in no uncertain terms, 'You think you know something important, don't you? Well, you don't.'

I learned many critical lessons in three relationships within six years, and I know there are still more lessons and insights to come. What were some of these necessary and insightful teachings?

Firstly, don't mistake feeling sorry for someone for love. I had done this at least twice, which was a big mistake.

Secondly, don't mistake lust for love. Unless we have a close friendship *and* a physical attraction, it isn't love, no matter what the media, our partner or our parents' generation might have us believe.

Thirdly, don't idealise relationships. Don't think that just because you feel you have committed to someone, you should ever tolerate abuse. If we can't treat each other with respect in our relationships, we must either find a way to restore it or leave.

Fourthly, don't lose yourself. My problem with having had the transcendent experience was that I was trying to rewrite myself, to change the person I was into someone calmer and more content – to overcome the triggers and traumas of my past. But my minimal identity had been compromised in all the relationships, especially the last one. If a relationship's price is the genuine you, the price is too high.

There were many other lessons learned from these relationships. I soon realised my whole life – especially childhood – had been focused in such a way that having a satisfying relationship would always have been a slim possibility from the outset, requiring a massive effort to ever make work.

I tried dating for a bit, then lost interest – it was all too difficult. However, I was finding satisfaction and progressing in other aspects of life.

From these relationships, I also learned critical lessons about feelings and some profound insights that could be explored within romantic love. In chapter 11, we will learn how to use feelings to understand romantic love.

During the first relationship, I began to write a book – science fiction at first. When I was in the last and most traumatic relationship, I couldn't write, partly because I had no time since I was working full-time, and doing most of the housework and cooking. Once it ended, I returned to writing and found it immensely therapeutic. I was starting to delve deep once again into the human heart.

To my great surprise, writing led me to make the most profound serendipitous discovery about desires and feelings I'd ever made.

CHAPTER 6

THE BALANCE OF SELF MODEL – HUMANITY'S HEART REVEALED?

The air was peaceful, humid, filled with echoing spikes of melodious birdsong. Underfoot, off the unpaved meandering paths and narrow gravel roads, was a salad of curled bark, dried eucalypt leaves and short scrub framed by trees of varying eras – many ancient plant-based beings lived here. The aroma was unfamiliar and more subtle than the country of my younger self. It felt different from down south, calming, yet with its own unique spirit. Nestled among the natural woodland were buildings – scattered, makeshift and almost random. Under a small shelter was a giant bronzed bell with Sanskrit symbols. I had visited the Chenrezig Institute near Eudlo, inland from the Sunshine Coast, a few times, as I was still curious about Tibetan Buddhist beliefs and taken by the general peace of the place. I had the setting for my new book.

It was set almost eighty years in the future. Another institute was nestled in a similar landscape, but much more extensive and ordered. At its centre was a large prominent building with an imposing sandstone entrance. Other buildings were scattered around the central circular enclosed space as if branching out from the centre of a spider's web – all paths and roads led to the focus. The forest was still close; trees and grassland were blended seamlessly among the human-built structures as if part of the natural vista, absorbing and sharing its heart. An upside-down triangle was carved into the grand entry's brown, textured, ancient rock, with words carved at each spike. At the bottom, the word 'SELF'. To the upper left 'FAMILY', and the upper right, in much larger letters, the word 'COMMUNITY'. In the centre was a circular representation of the Earth.

This centre was The Institute of Mind, prominent in research and teaching, with similar institutes scattered worldwide. By this point in time, many people had sorted the fundamentals of how mind, body and beyond connected and worked – a framework of understanding had emerged that allowed for individual self-realisation, scientific correlation and discovery occurring side-by-side. In addition, the Institute and other research centres were finalising the physics for travelling beyond the stars to the point of making it work. It was an era of awakening and promise, with glimpses of possible lasting peace, reaching to the stars and much further. The anti-hero, however, had other plans.

I imagined one of the elites – highly trained by the Institute, troubled with past traumas unresolved and wanting the Institute and all similar organisations brought down – had gone rogue. The knowledge he held gave him the means to manipulate and potentially dominate the world. With a deep understanding of what drove us as human beings – our fears and desires – and with emerging technology that offered limitless energy, he was out for revenge and power. I imagined him starting in advertising and media since he knew how to manipulate people at a level previously unseen and profit from it. Only a person of similar skill and knowledge could stop him.

This book was my second work of fiction. Unfortunately, my agent hadn't found a home with a publisher for my first. Although it was action driven, the regular comment in the rejection letters was that the story was weak. Looking back, they were right – the character didn't grow and become transformed by her experiences enough to be a satisfying read. I was considering writing a new book when my agent suddenly died of stomach cancer. After that, the relationships happened – and with the last failed relationship behind me, inspiration returned. As part of my writing therapy, I wrote a screenplay about drug companies ruling the world. After I reconciled that a movie wasn't what I wanted to dominate my next five years, I wrote a new work – and the Institute of Mind scenario was born. Then it struck me the sign above the community centre could have positive potential in the real world. This sign above the archway was part of a puzzle I had been searching for. Had the fundamental essence of humanity's heart revealed itself?

The struggling mothers I saw as a GP had heavily influenced the idea of the upside-down triangle above the community hall entrance. Mums would come in, distressed, crying, unable to cope, asking what was wrong with them. Most were depressed. Their anxiety and stress levels were often through the roof. I had to stop asking if they got any time for themselves, because so many of them would burst into tears or say cynically, 'What's that?' These were mothers driven to the limit, looking after the kids, doing the housework, often in full-time jobs, and trying to maintain their relationships. Where was their life balance? There wasn't any.

It became evident we all need time for ourselves. We all need time for our children and partners. We all need time with our friends and to maintain social connections. Work for many women and men would be their only significant time for socialising. Many would easily get caught up in extremes of one area but neglect the others.

For example, if they stayed home to focus on raising the children, mums would often struggle to find friends – many of their friends were working and didn't have the time to catch up. Many guys, if they worked long hours, would only have a connection with people at work and then come home exhausted and offer what energy they had left to their children – their wife getting only the scraps of energy remaining. If the guys were particularly stressed or found the home environment too much, they would stay at work – defining themselves as workers and providers. Single parents were worse off; it was working, then kids, and not much else. To ask any of them when they had last done something just for themselves, or when their last date night was with just their partner, feelings of worthlessness, failure and guilt would soon reveal themselves.

I designed the upside-down triangle diagram as a simple example of how we should balance our time. It became far more valuable and insightful than I had ever imagined.

I called it The Balance of Self Model. As I contemplated its components, it revealed a potential power for positive change so commanding I couldn't believe it. This was a 'holy crap' moment; the idea and insight were startling yet simple. Was this also a summary of the essence of humanity's heart I had searched for? If it was, it was a serendipitous discovery.

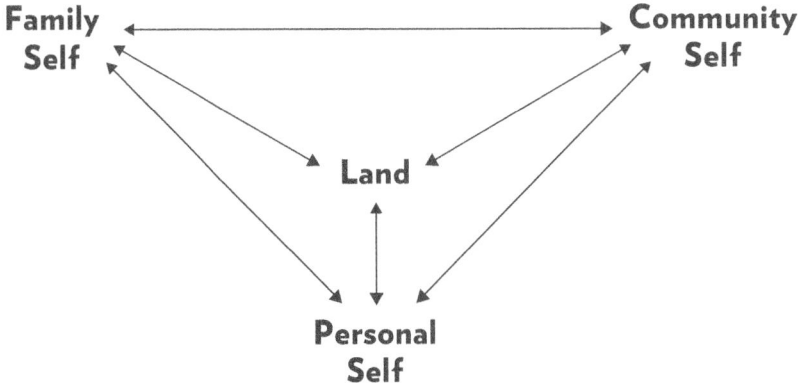

You will recall that, soon after my transcendent experience with The All, I tried to make sense of the basics of the human mind and heart to find the essence of our humanity that set us apart from other beings. Desires – motivations – were key. Human desires and what satisfied them were specific to humans. They set us apart and defined us, ensuring we would find our place in nature's tapestry. Could this simple diagram help answer the question of what are our basic human desires were and put names to them? After all, if we knew what they were, we could learn to satisfy them. We could understand what we needed to do to be satisfied, balanced human beings.

At the core of the diagram was 'Land'. Land, for me, represented nature. I put it there to reflect how critical nature was to help me discover and realise my sense of genuine self – such as the time meditating under the tree near my parents' farm during uni break. But Land/Nature/Country was far more fundamental. I soon realised it was the core of our being that influenced every aspect of our desires. Land grounded us and helped us recognise the human essences that stemmed from it – we were of the Land. So Land/Country/Nature was at the centre of the diagram where it should rightfully be –

a guide and source of enormous self-insight and wisdom if we were prepared to listen.

Rather than SELF, FAMILY, COMMUNITY, as I'd had written above the archway to the community centre in the fictional book, I changed the names to 'Personal Self', 'Family Self', and 'Community Self'. Why the change? The diagram was no longer just a recognition of how we should balance our time; it was how we should balance our hearts. Every component was now a part of our overall self.

The diagram reminded me of the Rosetta Stone of our hearts. It helped translate for us what our hearts desired and why we might feel as we do – make sense of what we feel. Almost immediately, I also realised the model's enormous potential to help resolve and prevent depression.

Depression – a revelation

I had almost no practical understanding of my long-lasting depression through high school and most of university. I truly believed what the psychiatrists taught us in medical school, that a chemical imbalance caused depression in the brain. The treatment these people needed was medication. How wrong I had been.

Many clients I see find the side effects of antidepressant medication intolerable. Others welcome the medication's emotional numbing feeling as it allows them to return to work and function – at least for a while. All these struggling mothers were asking me for medications, afraid they were failing where other mothers seemed to succeed. If they'd asked the other women around them, they'd have soon found out how many of them were, sadly, on antidepressants – over a third of them or more. As I pondered The Balance of Self (BOS) Model, suddenly, depression seemed to make sense; it wasn't a chemical problem. To understand depression was to recognise how nature made us, crying out for us to satisfy our most elemental humanity.

When a client presents to me as a GP seeking help for their depression, I assess them, ensure there is no physical trigger such as an underactive thyroid, and ensure they are safe and of no risk to themselves or others. I then offer them counselling with me or a referral to a psychologist. If the illness is life-threatening, hospital admission can be lifesaving. If they return for counselling, I will often discuss depression in the following way.

I begin by asking them what they have heard or read about the causes of depression. For example, they might bring up the notion that it results from a chemical imbalance in the brain. In that case, I acknowledge I once believed that too and then present clear evidence this isn't true. For starters, the brain is dynamic and plastic change what you think, and you rewire the brain and change its brain chemistry. I then introduce the biopsychosocial model, which is a holistic model that considers influences such as biology, psychology and social environment on mental health. Medicine, I explain, doesn't understand depression very well, but it has worked out many helpful strategies. I then mention my bias; I prefer not to use medications except as a last resort. Often, by now, they know this as my bias since it is highlighted in my profile for the practice online.

Then I explain how I see depression differently, acknowledging that these ideas don't come from scientific research or studies.

Human beings, I explain, were made to survive in the natural world. Nature gave us a set of primary motivations or desires to ensure we meet our basic human needs and can thrive in the natural world. Such desires include hunger, thirst, the need for shelter, community and having a family. I would then ask them a question along the lines of – 'How do you think we feel if we meet these basic desires?'

Most of them answer they would feel good or satisfied.

Exactly, it's as if nature is patting us on the back and saying, please do more of that.

I would then ask how they might feel if those basic needs were not met.

The usual reply is, 'Crap.' I'm happy to go along with that.

The real trick to understanding depression, I then explain, is to recognise our brain is made to always predict the future. Why does it do that? There is a survival advantage to knowing what might happen before it does. If we can predict the lion is around the next corner, we can avoid it. Anticipating what might happen can help keep us alive. How does our brain predict the future? It assumes.

Our brain assumes what happened before will happen again – we know these assumptions as memories. It then jumbles up the memories, extrapolates some of them, and combines them to create what we know as stories or narratives. Stories about us, who we are and how others will treat us. Stories about the world and what we might expect to befall us. Day or night, whether consciously aware of it or not, our brain is creating stories about us and our future – how we can get our needs met and what that might look like, trying to satisfy us as human beings.

Now, I would continue, suppose the stories of the future our brain creates project ahead and see that one of our essential needs won't get met. How will that make us feel?

The usual reply is, 'Crap.'

Suppose our narratives of the future predict we won't have any of our needs met. 'How will that feel?' I'd ask.

'Very crap,' some would reply. Others might say, 'Depressed'.

We may know this feeling as hopelessness. We can now create a new definition of hopelessness. Hopelessness is when we can't see how virtually any of our basic human needs will be met.

'One of the commonest things I find among people who are depressed,' I tell them, 'is feeling trapped.'

The mothers I see coming in struggling, the guys overworked and over-committed, the children alone and emotionally neglected, can all feel trapped – there is no way out. There is no way to have their basic human needs met.

The other way I might explain depression is more scientific. I explain that our brain is simulating the future to lay down pathways – nerve connections – to prepare us so we know what to do if it happens – like a rehearsal. If the simulation it runs doesn't see how its needs get met, we notice those feelings as sadness. When the negative projections into the future show no signs of letting up, we know it as such a profound sense of hopelessness that we feel depressed.

Almost everyone who suffers from depression relates to these explanations very well – they seem to resonate.

The key, then, I would continue, is to understand these basic needs because if we know what they are, we can actively work to satisfy them – to give ourselves hope.

What are the basic human needs? I would then present the BOS Model, explain its components and how it works.

Personal Self, I would explain, is a summary of all the desires that keep us alive in our own right, such as hunger, thirst and need for shelter. But Personal Self is much more. It also represents the genuine self – what you feel is truly deep inside you that the influence of others hasn't corrupted. An example I use to help give a sense of the level of

Personal Self is to ask them to imagine being the only person on the planet with no one to answer to. What do you like? What would you like to do? The aim is not to imagine a zombie apocalypse as much as to ask what you would like if there was no one to notice or impress. Do you know? Almost everyone who suffers from depression struggles to answer this question – suggestive that they have lost contact with the honest desires of their heart as I had for most of my younger years until realising The All.

But the Personal Self is so much more; it is having a strong sense of choice – self-empowerment. It is self-respect – keeping our body and mind healthy. It is about solid self-worth – not always putting our needs at the bottom of our list of priorities. And it is about being our own best friend. How many of us talk badly to ourselves in a way a best friend never would? Being our best friend is about care, kindness, understanding, empathy and compassion for yourself. Would you treat your best friend the way you have come to treat yourself, I would often ask? The answer is almost universally, 'No'.

Family Self, I would continue, summarises all the desires that drive us to be part of families and perhaps have a family of our own – no babies, no humanity. Men and women can expect to have different desires here or they would be doing the same tasks. In the natural world, nature defined what qualities we would find attractive and necessary in each other to give our children the best chance of survival. To satisfy Family Self needs is to ensure a close and mutually satisfying relationship and that children's emotional and physical needs are satisfied. It is to maintain a greater family connection, so our children have more role models and greater loving and caring support.

Community Self summarises all the desires that drive us together to form supportive collectives. I have often asked clients whether humans would survive better in nature alone or in groups. We survive better in groups. We are a social species; social connection is deeply ingrained. Not having a sense of care and support around us can quickly leave us feeling the deep hollowness of loneliness, being different, not fitting in, being excluded and being unloved. These are the feelings I suffered when I was ostracised at school, though I have noticed many have suffered the pains of exclusion much worse than me. The pains of low Community Self can be especially powerful in adolescence.

I would then briefly explain the place of Land in the middle of the diagram and how it affects the expression of all our desires, such as our sense of self, family sizes and culture. Nature and the Country around us determine our language, stories, what we eat and how we treat each other. Not everyone in the city gets the potential benefits of connecting with nature. Those who have grown up rurally, like I did, quickly do.

I explain that the diagram has arrows linking everything to remind us that all the components affect each other and ultimately come together as a whole. The whole is greater than the sum of its parts.

What about how the model applies to us today? Most of us no longer live in the natural world.

I admit it took me a while, but eventually, I realised the desires summarised in the diagram were our needs when we were tribal. In the tribe, men often hung around men and women around women. Children would be wherever they could get attention, knowing everyone cared for and loved them.

Would women in a tribe be left alone with the children, isolated from everyone and have no say in the goings on around them? Rarely, since everyone recognised it took the tribe to raise the child.

The mothers needed great support from everyone to do the most important job – ensuring the care and well-being of those who came after them.

How long did we live such tribal lives? Our desires evolved over millions of years. We have only lived in civilisations beyond that of tribal nomads for approximately five-and-a-half to six thousand years. Can we expect all those desires that evolved over millions of years to disappear in just a few thousand years?

'No' would be the obvious answer.

Nature placed inside us desires refined over millions of years to find satisfaction in balance with the natural world. Instead, we now live in concrete canyons of many millions. We no longer have the close, supportive, physical connection of our tribe. The basics of our humanity, the essences that make us who we are in this world, often aren't being met, and many of us – unsurprisingly – can't see how they will be met. How are we expected to feel?

Depressed, alone and unsatisfied? Disconnected? Stressed unnecessarily?

Why do I explain depression in these terms? For several reasons. One is to help people see how they can restore balance. Another is to remind us depression isn't our fault.

In a world where success becomes measured in material assets and status – how much you own, what suburb you live in, the size of your house, and what job you work in – it is easy to feel inadequate and left behind. It is easy to feel the only reason we aren't as well off as others and happy like them is that there is something wrong with us – we aren't normal.

We are normal. We feel as we expect we would under the conditions and priorities we have placed on ourselves.

Further insights from The Balance of Self Model

The BOS Model was a revelation. It offered far more than I had hoped, and it kept giving.

For instance, some other valuable insights I noticed we could gain from the model include the following:

- We all need self-time to enhance our connection with ourselves – and beyond – to feel at peace and truly fulfilled.
- Self does not have to equal selfishness. We will discuss this more later in chapter 10.
- Children are precious and critical – their well-being should be our priority, especially their emotional well-being. It isn't the extra physical stuff they need from us as much as attention, caring, nurturing and love. They need their tribe.
- Relationships need care and focus too. In the tribe, there were plenty of babysitters.
- We need our girlfriends and mates.
- We all seek a greater community that listens, treats us respectfully and cares for and protects us.
- To connect with nature is to be reminded of the essence of our humanity – the desires that nature instilled in us to find balance and harmony within its embrace.

- The model is a functional model, not a recipe to follow or a hierarchy of things to achieve. The aim is to find balance. No two people are alike, so the balance we need and what that looks like in our life will differ from how that may look for others.

The BOS Model is a window into our hearts; it empowers us.

At the same time, the model reaffirms the essence of our humanity.

It would take me ten years to write my first non-fiction work, *A Balance of Self – a new approach to self-understanding, lasting happiness and self-truth*. It wasn't written as a feel-good book to have mass appeal, but I felt I needed to write it. However, it teaches us how the BOS Model works and how to fix some imbalances. It also reminds us of a vast potential weakness in us all that can threaten our future.

Awake or asleep, our brain uses past experiences to create a biological representation of what might happen; it creates nerve connections that try to reflect possible futures. We may know these connections as our brain creating stories or narratives of what might happen to help us avoid danger, and see what path we need to take to meet our basic human needs. For instance, have you noticed your mind coming up with worst case scenarios of all the things that might go wrong and scaring you, or rehearsing what you will say before you make a phone call? Worrying about worst cases and rehearsal in our mind before an event are a clear example of our brain running simulations of what might happen. In essence, our brain constantly runs simulations.

However, the brain's simulator, I realised, has a vast potential flaw. It needs help distinguishing reality from fantasy.

What is the brain's simulator?

You will recall, our brain creates possible futures using memories of past experiences that have become laid down as nerve connections so we are prepared. In other words, it constantly simulates what might be – it acts as a simulator. But, has the past ever happened the same again? No. So we can be sure it is just making up fantasies. Every fantasy is likely to be more inaccurate with the more assumptions it makes. The further it tries to peer into the future, the less accurate we can expect it to be.

In essence, we are living out our brain's dreaming.

The problem is our brain doesn't know which dreams are realistic or which aren't. So it waits to see which one appears to come true, then holds onto it. To help us from being too lost in fantasy, it uses two primary reality checks: nature and each other.

Nature is a tremendous and direct reality check. For example, we believe we can live only off the earth's energy and nothing else. In that case, the world's physical nature will see us die of thirst and hunger. Likewise, if we don't believe as a people that we should have sex because we are 'higher' beings, then we become extinct. Nature is a forthright and honest reality tester.

But we also live in groups. We must think alike and hold similar stories to bond better and be more effective and cohesive. Fundamentally, we should maintain similar morals, ethics, dreamings and beliefs. But take us away from nature and where is our grounding? All we have is fantasy-prone minds bouncing off each other.

Detach from nature, and we can begin to believe almost anything we like, anything that feels good, so long as others also believe it. Our beliefs, stories and dreams can quickly get us out of balance with nature and the natural desires in each of us, and we can lose connection with morals and ethics that work. We can lose our way, feel terrible, see atrocities around us, treat each other horribly and have no idea why. Our stories, dreams and fantasies can become dysfunctional, and we won't even realise it.

Our ability to disconnect from the real world – reality – so easily, makes finding a balance of self as set out in the BOS Model so critical. The model is grounded in nature. It asks us to search for the inner truth of the essence of our humanity – what it is to be human, functional, sustainable, balanced with each other and nature, and if we believe in it, in balance with The All.

When I first discovered the BOS Model, I had no idea it offered more than a simple framework to help balance our lives. As I looked deeper, I saw so many other insights and possibilities. The model was like the trunk of a tree, with so many branches and twigs and leaves of discovery flourishing and continuing to grow from it. As a psychologist colleague recently reminded me, the model has stayed the test of time for over fifteen years – its basic approach and insights still seem to help others quite well. So if nothing else, the model can be helpful.

By this point, I was still unsure about relationships, especially what fundamentals were necessary for them to work. In my reflections, I wondered, could men and women have lasting, stable, satisfying relationships if they aren't in connection with their hearts? The BOS Model reminded me how important it was to be true to our hearts to find lasting satisfaction. My focus turned to women, many of whom seemed to be torn away from their hearts and struggling. I began to research tribal cultures throughout history and discovered that women who had lived in mostly peaceful societies were revered for their role as women. However, that's not the case today. Cultures worldwide are still treating women as second-rate and disrespecting them. What happened? What changed?

My questioning sent me on a meditative and research path to better understand the fundamentals at the core of any stable, satisfying relationship – our basic needs in relationships. But, more importantly, how did women fall from such grace, and should we aim to reinstate women who are true to their hearts with much higher status than we currently do?

These are questions that offer important insights into many fundamental feelings. They would also help uncover vital clues about how we created a world filled with unnecessary misery – how we destroyed so much balance, and why we still suffer from it today.

CHAPTER 7

WOMEN POWER – A CURE WE NEED?

In the origin tale of the Keres-speaking Laguna Pueblo Indians of North America, Thought Woman – also known as Spider Old Woman, Spider-Woman or the wisdom keeper – is considered the spirit of creation, the supreme spirit. She is the spirit woman who brought life, balance and the ability to make our own decisions to humanity as opposed to ruling over us and punishing us if we didn't do what was decreed. The Keres Indians believe Thought Woman will return and help restore balance to the world. It was the spirit of these ancient women of the past, who were respected, acknowledged and empowered with the ability to transform a society, that engendered the vision of my next book, *The Fall and Rise of Women, How Women Can Change the World*.

Why would I try to elevate the spirit of ancient women?

In any image of a future peaceful, balanced, harmonious, stable and sustainable society, I knew women being true to their heart would be critical – for reasons that will become apparent shortly. Writing this book would also be an excellent opportunity for personal healing from past relationships – to understand what went wrong and better understand relationships at their core. The writing and meditation involved would help me to make greater sense of the desires – and feelings – of Family Self in the BOS Model. A common complaint between the genders soon became apparent.

Several women I was reading about in the media were saying men needed to grow a pair; that men had become too soft, indecisive, submissive and unappealing. More than a few women I was seeing in my practice made similar comments. Men complained, too. Many men were upset at how hard it was to find a caring, supportive, feminine woman to settle down with. What was going on? Was I missing something pivotal here? The quandary sent me questioning and theorising. Could there be fundamental traits nature explicitly created for each gender that the opposite sex found attractive? If so, what might some of these characteristics look like? And could we ever expect to have truly satisfied relationships if we didn't meet these basics?

In other words, had we lost our way as men and women – a connection to the essence of our feminine and masculine being? Was that loss contributing to relationship dissatisfaction? In a time when even to mention gender is to be pilloried – gender is a social construct of society, didn't you know? – I needed to look deeper than what was becoming popular and see if there was something with substance we could personally tap into.

Do you think gender and gender roles are real? Gender and gender roles are a controversial topic, considering a significant number of people are fluid in gender identity or don't regard gender in hetero-normative terms. I knew I could be completely wrong about what gender roles are altogether.

I began to research as well as explore within.

Immediately, a stark realisation struck me. Men and women needed to be attracted to each other and find significant contentment and fulfilment in each other's company for a relationship to work. Sure, some variations of mutual attraction would exist and, no doubt, bring satisfaction to the people concerned. Still, the bottom line is that most women would need to want to be with a man, and vice versa, and together they would need to be satisfied enough not to leave. Why would this need to be the case? Otherwise, there would be no babies and/or the children would be at risk if the family broke up before they were ready to take on adult roles.

Were there perhaps, I wondered, womanly or feminine traits that were true to women's hearts that would ensure our families and children thrive? Traits that would also extend to enhance the caring and well-being of everyone in a community, including the elderly and infirm?

The lives of ancient tribes who were under the greater influence of nature drew me to search for insights into life before we developed civilisation. What I discovered left me both shocked and dismayed.

Behind the bias of anthropologists – mostly men imposing their white, privileged, modern world prejudices – I found in several ancient tribes that women were revered, at the very least holding significant power and influence. I found many examples of this in ancient North American cultures, such as the Navaho, Keres-speaking, Cherokee, and Lakota tribes and within the Iroquois Nation or Confederacy south of the Great Lakes before the arrival of Europeans. In other countries, I could find evidence of powerful central female gods and spirits. It seemed if the people mainly lived peaceful, stable lives, then women were often revered and highly respected to the point of – in some cases – being deified. I contrasted this with how women are treated today and felt immense sadness.

How could this happen? How could women be revered in some ancient tribal cultures, yet, in virtually all other civilisations throughout history, be treated as second-class citizens and so easily defiled? Even the Sumerian civilisation dating back over five and half thousand years, often regarded as the first civilisation, had made women second to men, controlling what they wore and their ability to own property.

I sought the simplest yet most practical answer I could. Finally, I returned to reflecting on our basic human desires to see if they offered any insights.

It was apparent that nature would have to give us gender-defined roles that suited our biological–physical differences to survive and thrive in the natural world. Men, for instance, couldn't breastfeed, and babies are born so fragile and dependent, a close bond with their mother would be critical. In addition, men were often larger and more robust than their female counterparts, with more physical endurance, ideal for hunting and defending the family and tribe.

What gender roles might nature have defined in nomadic tribal humankind?

What if women were primarily driven to be carers and nurturers and men were to provide and protect? That way, by women focusing on caring and nurturing the young and everyone else in the tribe, we had solid foundations for feeling loved, cared for and belonging. With men concentrating on supporting the women and children by hunting and defending them, it gave everyone a sense of safety and security, knowing we were loved by being well provided for and kept safe.

In short, let us assume for the moment that the primary distinguishing desires of each gender would drive women to be carers and nurturers and men to provide and protect. This distinction is just an assumption. It is not saying that every woman or man would fully embrace these gender-related desires in a tribe, only that there is sufficient tendency towards doing so. After all, embracing our physical gender differences holds a recognisable survival advantage in many places in the natural world.

But as the BOS Model reminded me, desires are dynamic; they change according to our needs at any time. For instance, we may be hungry when we meet the partner of our dreams. Do we then suppress the hunger so we can meet them? Or do we miss out on a great match with a love that could endure because we are famished and like burgers? So our desires flow and change according to our circumstances and needs.

I wondered further what might happen if our tribe was attacked; how might our desire profile change then?

When under the attack of another tribe, which desires would rise within us? Would it be the desire to care and nurture or those to provide and protect?

Clearly, under attack, the desire to protect would rise in all of us, even the women, who can be formidable opponents. However, once we dismiss the enemy, women can let caring and nurturing desires dominate, so they can better do the most critical job – raising our children, the next generation.

But what happens to these desires if we are almost constantly threatened or attacked?

Then our desire to provide and protect would rise over long periods. Suppose our desire to care and nurture are recognised as most valuable and worthy of support in times of peace and stability. In that case, we will value the desire to provide and protect more in times of constant threat.

In other words, nature says first, I keep you alive, then you can do the caring and nurturing after that. We can't care for children if they or we are dead.

How might we expect a change in the profile of desire in a society under constant threat to affect how we treat women in society?

It would hardly be surprising that in stable peacetime, the innate caring and nurturing qualities of women would see women highly respected and even revered. But when the society or tribe is under constant threat, the role of provider and protector would be most reputable and held in the highest regard.

So, if women want to be respected and valued in a society under constant threat, they must focus on becoming providers and protectors or at least take on these traits. In other words, to behave more like men and suppress any innate feminine calling.

In other words, if we create a society that is insecure, unsafe and constantly struggling to survive, we can expect a world dominated by men, where being a woman is considered inferior.

Sound familiar?

Think about how we live today. Do we live in safe and secure societies driven primarily to care for each other and satisfy the growing hearts of our children? Or do we live in a community of competitors, unsure who has our back, struggling to get ahead and making raising children a secondary priority? So we give the job of raising them to someone else – hence, paid childcare.

We live in a world dominated by the primary desire of men to provide and protect; we live in a world of gender imbalance.

But this isn't how it was supposed to or has to be. Nature balanced men's desires with women's desires. It made us such that the potentially destructive desires inherent in men were countered and contained by the peaceful, caring and settling desires innate in women.

Like it or not, the bottom line is the desire to provide and protect promotes fighting. As we compete for limited food and resources and protect our territory, we often fight for them. It is then better to take over the land of our competitor for two good reasons, so they don't threaten us, and so there is plenty for our families.

In contrast, the desire to care and nurture doesn't want us to fight – fighting and unnecessary expansion threaten our families' lives, and we could all be killed or constantly attacked. By their very nature, the desire for caring and nurturing promotes peace and stability. With women in positions of influence, we could contain the desire to provide and protect enough to create lasting peace.

Look to a time when we lived closer to nature. We can easily recognise the desires of men and women were supposed to be at least equal in power and influence, or better still, the natural desires inherent in women were better suited to ensure peace and balance.

Suppose our priority is to create lasting peace and restore balance and sustainability. In that case, it soon becomes apparent that women faithful to their hearts and connected to nature are critical.

But don't tell me this nonsense that women should be carers and nurturers; you are just another man trying to oppress them and keep them in the home.

Am I? Does promoting women being true to their feminine hearts mean they should have no power and be kept isolated and a man's servant?

I don't believe it does. An ancient North American culture found a promising way for women to have great power and still be true to their hearts centuries before Europeans arrived.

It is estimated that sometime in the early to mid-15th century AD, perhaps earlier, the Great Peacemaker, along with Jigonhsasse – a woman – and Hiawatha – a leader of the Onondaga people, the Mohawk people or both – negotiated to create what would be called the Iroquois Confederacy. What was once five warring tribes would be united at a counsel table to vote on matters of importance. Only men could sit at the table and represent their people. But women owned the seat and chose the man to represent them. If the man broke counsel rules or they no longer considered him to be acting in their tribe's best interest, the women would replace him. In essence, women held real power behind the scenes.

This unique form of governance created stability and peace for centuries until the arrival of the white man. The council structure was said to be the inspiration for the new government of the fledgling United States of America.

In today's terms, their solution was simple: only women could vote, but they could only vote for men. It would mean more women in places of influence and their counsel sought after for their wisdom, ideally achieved through a greater connection with nature and their inner – ancient tribal woman – self.

By recommending women connect more with their hearts, I am in no way implying we should oppress women in any way – quite the opposite. I believe women close to their hearts should have much greater power than they do today.

Does that mean gender roles should exist, or are they outdated?

That remains a difficult question. So let me turn the question around to help us understand it. First, suppose caring and nurturing were considered the most valued activities and roles. In those circumstances, women were highly respected and viewed more than the equal of any man. As a result, they held great power in these activities and within society. And society was community orientated as a result – more connected. Would we still be debating gender roles? And would so many women be driven to make money and have power? Would our mortgage be more important than our time meeting the emotional needs of our children?

In other words, how much of the gender role debate is because women are unappreciated, undervalued and not respected if they prefer caring roles, such as staying home to care for the children? And when at home, they have almost no social connection or influence or are considered worthy of being heard.

When did gender equality mean being a provider or protector like a man?

Of course, women should be allowed to choose whatever role they like. However, how differently would we view gender roles if we didn't live in societies under chronic threat and dominated by the primary desires inherent in men?

I still consider gender roles useful, provided we regard them as being of equal value, for the following reasons.

Firstly, it allows us to return closer to the nature-defined roles of our biology. For example, it means women can explore and feel validated in discovering and realising the feminine self. They can connect with the ancient tribal essence of being a woman. Similarly, it means men too can explore their masculine selves and feel valued and supported in realising these roles as men respectful of women and each other at all times – realising their functional masculine selves. This level of respect is critical. We can feel more in tune with our deeper selves and not feel pressured by society or anyone else to conform to their views of who they believe we should be.

Secondly, by following closer to nature-defined gender roles, we make it easier for our adolescents to find their place as adults within our society as men and women. Yes, they can explore their masculine and feminine natures. But once they choose, what we expect of them will be apparent, especially regarding respecting the opposite sex.

Once, we had coming-of-age ceremonies to help with the difficult transition into adulthood that would clarify our roles and expectation of society as men and women. Sadly, such rituals are few and far between today. Now we expect our young men and women to explore and find out where they fit, unguided and alone. The gender role debate is making it much harder for our youth than it needs to be to feel valued and accepted in our communities.

The gender role debate is making it harder for all of us. Men are abandoning their masculinity and being abused by women for being too soft. Likewise, women abandon their femininity, fearing being too weak, disrespected and labelled as not feminine enough will make them somehow less valuable, capable and employable.

What a sad and confusing state of affairs. But, unfortunately, chronic threats and civilisation have much to answer for.

When I wrote *The Fall and Rise of Women, How Women Can Change the World,* I didn't write it with the intention of telling women who or what they should be, as much to recommend that they listen less to men and society and more to the positive support of other women – the deeper spiritual ancient womanly tribal heart – and gain greater wisdom through a closer connection with nature. Ultimately, what women – or any of us – decide to be or to explore is up to them. No matter our gender choice or role, we still need to respect, care for and listen to each other.

The Fall and Rise of Women also includes many common-sense lessons and summarises the basic needs of any relationship, so we can build upon stronger foundations from the start. In addition, there are many feelings to explore related to gender and being a woman or a man.

In a world dominated by the out-of-control destructive desires of men, what hope do we have of balancing the aggression and brutal competition innate and often dominant in men if not even women are prepared to consider listening more to their caring and nurturing hearts? So perhaps we do need Thought Woman to return, as the Keres-speaking Indians remind us, to help restore balance after all.

As I began researching women's fall, I accidentally suddenly glimpsed upon perhaps the three most destructive human desires nature has ever created: the desire for wealth, power and status. I soon discovered that unless we learned to counter or contain them, we weren't just threatening the world with ongoing catastrophic imbalance and misery; we were putting all life on the planet at risk. Until then, I had no idea that just a few simple human desires could be so profoundly universally toxic.

Thankfully, nature has also offered itself a way out – us.

These desires also began to explain why I didn't consider I had connected with God during my experience of The All. Had just three malevolent desires disconnected us from a purer connection with Him?

CHAPTER 8

DESIRES THAT BROKE THE WORLD

The antique, wooden-framed glass cabinets were pristine and scattered throughout the modest-sized lounge and dining rooms. The finest Royal Doulton gold-rimmed ceramic plates and figurines were proudly displayed in each dust-free cabinet. My mother and I had been invited to my sister's boyfriend's home for dinner, and the hostess (his mother) seemed pleased we noticed her collection. The boyfriend, G, was a nice chap, down to earth, red hair, one of two guys my sister hung around with in the same veterinary year. His father was the principal of one of the most prestigious schools in Sydney. The house on the outside seemed modest – two-story brick veneer – but the interior was filled with fine furniture and expensive pieces. Mum and I were on our best behaviour. This invitation was my first foray into the privilege of Sydney.

Lunch was impressive; the plates were high quality. The cutlery was different from your everyday draw-under-the-kitchen-sink variety. Conversation flowed. G's mother took the reins, and their glowing pride for him was soon obvious. Their other son was doing well, too.

He was a year ahead, studying medicine, and there were high hopes for him. Then we were privy to the local gossip, but none I'd ever experienced. It wasn't who was marrying who or what holidays they planned, but who they knew. Names of British Royalty sailed through the air – people I'd never thought of as particularly relevant. It was clear the crowd this proud lady sought to be associated with was of the highest class imaginable. I didn't know what to make of the nonchalant boasting.

Even as a six-year-old, my parents had taught me to behave well in case we dined out in a fine restaurant – good manners, how to eat, what cutlery to use. We dined out several times on a trip around the world back to Germany when I was six years old to visit family. The company paid for the trip, and I wore a blue three-piece suit most of the time, especially in Rome, where we visited St Peter's Square and the Colosseum. I had met wealthy people before, but not as an adult, nor in their home. We were middle-class, living in a rural setting where checking the weather for the week ahead was more important than what a privileged few might be doing overseas. These friendly people seemed quite at ease with the wealth and status they exemplified.

Even during this visit, I thought nothing of wealth, privilege and status – it was just how it was and how I knew it to be. That was until I understood what led to women's fall globally. Then, the global imbalance, destruction, mass inequality and much of our unnecessary suffering suddenly began to make disturbing sense. What had nature been thinking?

As you can tell by now, I make sense of human behaviours and feelings by better understanding the dynamics of human desires. For instance, I learned that our natural response to an environment of chronic threat seemed to have a toxic effect, especially for women seeking to be true to maternal, feminine desires. But there was more to the story of women's demise. Other potent desires were at play I had never recognised before, but which were always in plain sight.

Then came the breakthrough.

I asked myself, what other desires or situations would divide us? Naturally, the desire for friendship came to mind – especially since I was beginning to see friendship's social and clinical relevance. I noticed, for instance, that most of the people I saw with depression were depressed because of a lack of connection. We had become so competitive, friendships no longer seemed to be our priority. So not only was there a fall of women, but also a fall in friendship.

Then the penny dropped. Could the fall of women also be related to a fall in friendship?

Understanding desires and feelings, once again, held the clue.

How important was friendship to survival in tribal society, I wondered? It was vital. We may not have always seen eye to eye and liked everyone, but we always had each other's backs. Friendship desires such as wanting to feel valued, respected, cared for and protected – desires of Community Self – were like the glue of social connection. They offered us warm safety and security in our tribal world. Nature made the desire for friendship powerful inside us to ensure we thrived. So, what could break such powerful bonds?

The answer was agriculture.

Consider it for a moment – once we could grow our food on a plot of land, we didn't need others to ensure our family had enough; we had food security. When we were nomadic, having many hunters and gathers was effective – we could provide better for each other as a bigger group. But if we could grow our own fruits, vegetables and grains and tend our own animals, it would mean less dependence on others – less need for friendships.

From the point of view of desires, agriculture saw the rise of potent drives within us we probably never realised we had.

For instance, once we survive on a plot of land, we must grow more than one season's produce. The following season might be terrible, and if we don't have enough, then our family dies. To counter the problem, we need to grow excess. We know excess by another word, wealth.

Wealth brings a sense of security; the more we have, the more secure we can feel during hard times. So once we became farmers, we needed wealth.

By comparison, wealth in a nomadic tribe would be a useless burden. If you want it, you carry it.

'Honey, would you bring my twenty pairs of shoes?'

'No, you make new ones once we make camp.'

Develop agriculture, and we automatically create a strong desire inside us for wealth.

But now we have another problem, how can we keep our wealth?

Each farmer will grow and store a different amount. So, when the seasons are terrible, we can expect others to knock on our door and want our stuff. So, how can we stop them so our family still makes it through the tough times?

Suppose we have essential skills our community of farmers needs, such as leadership or healing skills. In that case, the others won't mind if we have more wealth than them because it is critical to the community that we survive.

In other words, if we have status, we have a better chance of keeping our wealth.

When we started farming, we also developed a stronger desire for status.

But what if we have no status? How else can we ensure we keep our much-needed excess?

We could buy the help of others to protect what we have. Or we could use force and take what we can from the weakest. Finally, we could form groups who take what they want and share it among a select few. We would use power to ensure our wealth is safe.

So, not only did the arrival of agriculture allow us to hunt no longer and roam to survive, but it also gave us a strong desire for wealth, status and power – a desire that would hardly appear in a stable, peaceful, tribal people living close to nature.

We often look back at our ancestors with some pride; the development of agriculture was a technological breakthrough. With farming, we could specialise in non-farming tasks such as making textiles, wine, masonry and writing. We could train professional armies that no longer had to farm to survive, so they could hone their skills and protect us. We could travel the world with our wealth and exchange it as merchants. Agriculture has changed the world, but our hearts are yet to reconcile with the change. When nature created just the right conditions to allow us to farm, it altered a profile of desire within us that would eventually threaten the fabric of nature itself.

How does knowing about the rise of desire for wealth, power and status help us understand the fall of women?

Consider the scenario of an agrarian society living in a region of unstable weather and rain. If seasons are regularly tricky, what can we expect that to do to our drive for wealth, power and status? They will go up.

Place us in a problematic geography with uncertain seasons, and we expect our desire for wealth, power and status to rise. Soon we can expect to fight among each other for what limited wealth is available as we all feel the pains of insecurity bite. Over time, we expect that a small group will own most of the wealth and have most of the privileges, and the majority will have much less. We know this as a hierarchy – the wealthy and powerful privileged few on top and everyone below them exploited, so the rich feel safe.

When we developed agriculture, we also created the foundations for the development of civilisations, always unequal, with the wealthy needing to exploit the less well-off to maintain their sense of safety and security.

How can we expect women to fare in such a hierarchical mix? Poorly. Why?

Does the desire for wealth, power and status better align with the desire for caring and nurturing or providing and protecting?

Civilisation, by its nature, is fuel to desires dominating the hearts of men. Men can now revel in the battle, the competition and the fight. Caring and nurturing in civilisations make us weak and vulnerable; they do not add to our security; they make us second-rate and easy to exploit by comparison. The person making a living and fighting the fights is king, not the person staying home caring for children.

The moment we created agricultural societies, the respect and value of women seeking to be true to their caring and nurturing hearts were under threat. And if women wanted to make it in our civilisations, they would have to adopt men's competitive, often ruthless qualities, and seek wealth, status and power.

The desires in our hearts inform us well. They show us that women do poorly if they live under conditions of chronic threat.

Our desires also show that women do poorly in agrarian hierarchical societies, where we are all driven to find security and safety at the top. Our communities have both chronic threats and brutal hierarchical male-driven dominant civilisations.

The fall of women was a sad inevitability.

But beginning to realise the nature of our desire for wealth, power and status also serendipitously revealed a force within us far more sinister than one to ensure women's fall.

Had I accidentally come up with the primary reason for so much imbalance, environmental destruction, oppression, wars, inequality, prejudice and hate? Was the source of our imbalanced hearts a natural reaction inside us? And if it was, could we do anything to stop it?

I scoured through history and current and recent events, and so much began to make sad and tragic sense. We were the instigators of misery and imbalance and exceptionally slow learners. We keep making the same mistakes.

Here is just a brief glimpse of what I discovered about how the influence of our desire for wealth, power and status has affected us personally, socially and globally, and promises to do worse still unless we learn to contain it.

Collapse of friendship

In a tribal society, we need friends to stay safe and alive. In a community driven by wealth, power and status, we don't need friends; we need allies to help and support us in our quest to accumulate wealth and influence. Friends, by definition, care for each other through thick and thin. What better expression of caring than sharing what we have to lessen someone else's burden and struggle? But we can't be extraordinarily wealthy and powerful if we keep giving away and sharing what we have.

This powerful desire for wealth, power and status divides us as a community, as we value friendship less and less. What we love more is the prominent home in the best suburb, the most expensive car, our children in the most exclusive schools, status jobs, and other shows of power and success.

This dominating desire for wealth and influence builds a lonely society struggling to know trust.

How many friends are you aware of who would still be your friend if you lost everything? How many friends could you truly trust?

Unsatisfying and unstable relationships

One of the great flashes of success in a society driven by wealth and influence is a good-looking, often youthful woman by a successful man's side. Compatibility? Who cares about that?

Most of us agree that the secret to a long and stable relationship is a close friendship. But, as we have seen, societies that are driven by wealth, power and status do not value true friendship. With women treated so poorly in a society driven by wealth, power and status, there is the temptation among women to find value, respect, acceptance, safety and security with a man who personifies material success. And men will search for who impresses on their arm. This is likely to be a lonely and distant relationship lacking the deep satisfaction of connection, and also to be fragile. Should her youth and beauty fade or his wealth be lost, they will cast each other aside.

A strong desire for wealth, power and status can also lead to financial and mortgage stress as people seek to 'get ahead'. Soon, both partners have to work long hours with less time for the kids and even less time for each other. But without regular, close time with a partner, how can friendship in a relationship last? Soon there will be bickering about being unable to pay the bills, further driving a wedge between them. Many relationships end because the family has decided the mortgage comes first, with the uncontrolled desire for wealth, power and status overriding the need for close connection.

People become property

The moment we created farms, we created wealth but also debt. If someone was starving, we could give them our extra produce on the promise of them paying us back. Often, the payment would be in the form of labour. If we wanted the cheapest work possible, they became debt or chattel enslaved people, bought and sold. People then came with a price just like livestock, an item without soul or feeling to be exchanged – property. Our desire for wealth, power and status makes human beings just another resource to exploit – it dehumanises us. The apparent extension of civilisation was always going to be slavery and exploitation.

Hierarchical civilisations were always going to create enslaved people. As a result, we see slavery develop across every continent, even in the earliest civilisations, independent of each other. We know slavery was rife in Europe, Asia, Africa and the Americas. Slavery still exists today, with the total number of enslaved people in modern times – such as debt and sex slaves – outnumbering those of earlier centuries.

When wealth, power and status dominate our hearts, we do not want to share; we want to exploit. The only way the wealthy and privileged can get and keep their extreme gains is by having cheap labour to achieve them. Unfortunately, the easiest and ripest to exploit are the weak, the desperate and those unable to fight back.

Are you in a job where profits are shared? Are you being exploited?

Nature defiled and climate under threat

Once we found equals among each other in our tribe, and by extension, we also treated nature with similar respect and reverence. We were part of something bigger than ourselves. We felt a bond with it similar to the connection we shared with our companions walking with us. Trees and creatures had spirits, a life we could emotionally connect to. When we started to use the land and its animals to accumulate wealth, all things in nature – and other people – were now simply another resource to exploit to satiate our wealth-driven desires. Nature and all within it were now emotionless, soulless objects and a means to an end. It is hard to exploit what you still find close to your heart. Desire for wealth, power and status blinded our hearts to any greater connection.

Worse still, our desire for wealth, power and status made us feel above nature. Our beliefs began to reflect this further, ensuring our more significant emotional disconnect.

Our stories once told of country and spiritual beings. Our spirits then morphed into gods that would answer us and do our bidding. We created temples, priests, priestesses and prophets to enhance our divine influence and the unquestioning loyalty of the people – who would dare question the will of a god or God?

From gods, we developed science and the power of technology. Our wars demanded we be technologically more advanced than our adversaries. Science ensured we detached even more from nature; then, we replaced the world of emotional connection with physical forces we could predict and manipulate. We *were* God, and nature was there to do our bidding.

When our primary aim is to accumulate unlimited wealth and power, we can quickly develop the belief that it is God's will – if we even admit He exists. Once our greed has God's blessing – it is God's will – of course, we will tear apart the land, over fish and pollute our seas, poison our land and have a climate impact. The bottom line is profit, not balance, harmony, sustainability or emotional connection. God is separate and controlling, just like us, and how we need to believe Him to be.

From the moment the desire for wealth, power and status arose, we would always disconnect from nature and the balance and insight it could offer us in return. We were always going to distance ourselves from The All.

Nature unwittingly gave us the means to farm – and has been paying for it ever since.

Endless wealth never satisfies

Human beings never do find lasting satisfaction and contentment in the accumulation of stuff. Instead, we realise it in the safety and security of each other – in people. That means our desire for wealth, power and status can never be satisfied because we can never reach the end goal – security and safety in connection. Ironically, the more we accumulate, the more insecure we become.

Fight to the top in a hierarchal civilisation, and do we feel safe and secure? Of course not; we are worried which of our rivals will take us down – for every Caesar, a Brutus lurks in the shadows. We are also worried that people will get wind of the con and rise up –

revolution – and topple us and our elite mates. But how do we quell the insecurities of unequal wealth and power? We seek more of them still, even if it means conquering other lands to get them.

Wealth, power and status are bottomless pits with a craving that can never be satiated. When the devotees answer these selfish cravings, they can be expected to compete with each other and ignore everyone else. If you aren't as wealthy and powerful as me, you are nothing; get out of my way. As the elite play this dreadful game with each other, they exploit, oppress, corrupt and are prepared to kill and cause untold damage along the way, as the desire for wealth, power and status is so influential and the fear of losing the gains so strong.

When the desire for wealth, power and status dominates a society, we can expect to be ruled by insecure fools with darkened hearts, unable or unwilling to change despite the misery within and all around them.

Empires, wars, repeat

Once the desire for wealth, power and status create and dominate a civilisation, we expect the civilisation to expand for the mentioned reasons – no wealth and power will be enough. If you don't want your people to be exploited and oppressed by an expanding empire, you will need another empire to stop it; nothing else will be powerful enough. Eventually, we can expect the rise of empires everywhere where the desire for wealth and power dominates, each threatening the other's selfish wealth and power-crazy elite.

History is filled with empires that rise, fall and are rebuilt. France was a classic example during the revolution in the 1700s. The French people cast the elite out, and some lost their heads. But then the greed we know as the desire for wealth, power and status was set free, no longer under the orderly control of one leader or aristocracy, and chaos ensued. So bad was the corruption and injustices spreading through France, it saw the rise of Napoleon Bonaparte and a new French empire that would try to conquer most of Europe, including Russia. Empire after empire came and went across Europe for thousands of years. It was similar in China.

China had empire after empire dating back thousands of years, the last falling in the early 20th century. The story was repetitive. An elite would fight to bring order among the brutal chaos of unbridled greed and inequality by creating an empire. Inevitably, the kingdom would be corrupted; ignore its people, exploit them and inequality would rise. Then there would be an uprising, and a new empire would be born – rinse and repeat.

From the British empire that ruled the world to the most powerful and expansive empire the world has ever known, the American Empire, we continue to create empires driven by greed. Today, other empires are forming or reforming to try to defend themselves from the threat posed by the greedy elite elsewhere, as in history. However, the desire for wealth, power and status creates wars and massive inequality within each empire's reach, and globally.

It is sad, yet not surprising; we have another war between empires in Europe, one in the Middle East, and the threat of another in Asia.

We need to be faster learners.

Authoritarianism and failed containment

Exploit the people, make them struggle to the point of desperation, then let them see the elite doing well and it will be hard to quell the expected unrest.

As we have seen, nature made human beings to be tribal. Tribal societies, for the most part, live by consensus – everyone has an equal say in matters affecting them all. Nature made us to feel heard and respected as equals. Exploit us to the point of impoverishment, no longer care what we say or feel, and take away any hope of reprieve, and you can expect the exploited to fight back. But fighting back threatens the privileged.

Many political devices have been employed to quell the chaos and contain the desire for wealth, power and status, and they all failed. China went to great lengths to develop intricate philosophies and beliefs to see if that would keep their empires stable – for example, Taoism, Confucianism and Buddhism and combinations of all three. They all failed.

In the West, we have tried democracy – at least we felt we had a say. But, unfortunately, that, too, has been corrupted to varying levels by those with the most significant wealth and power. Private companies and the profiteers who lead them, for instance, often have more ability to control government affairs than the people – the United States is a classic example of a democracy bought from under the people. So now, as inequality rises among many democracies, the people are naturally rising in response.

How do we suppress the uprising? First, we can use increased law and order – a crackdown on dissent. Chinese empires have tried that many times, but it didn't work. We can try a more decisive leader and dissolve the democracy – authoritarianism. That makes matters worse.

Initially, there may be a sense of order. Still, under an authoritarian regime, wealth, power and status rule unchallenged at the top. The exploited then have even less say and are ripe to be used even more.

What about Communism, where the government – the people – own the businesses? Suppose our desire for wealth, power and status remains. In that case, we can again expect a privileged elite to rule over others they can exploit. Communism is ripe for authoritarian rule; control the government, and you own all means of wealth creation and the people.

Wealth, power and status are desires that don't want to be controlled. They spread themselves freely and quickly. Even under the rule of the noblest leaders, we will inevitably see corruption rise and threaten peace and stability; our desire for wealth and power is that powerful and resilient. No political structure alone, be it democracy, Communism, tyranny or dictatorship, can fully contain them.

Recognising the influence and toxic nature of the uncontrolled desire for wealth, power and status offers answers to so much.

Look around for yourself – where can you see the desire for wealth, power and status causing struggle and harm in your life and society? How do you think these three malicious desires have changed the world? Has it been for the better?

When I visited my sister's boyfriend's home that day, I had no clue of the desire at play. Why speaking of royalty meant so much – status and connection with power likely played a big part. Why expensive items were something to be proud of and show off – displays of wealth and success were likely a strong influence. I didn't have the slightest clue when I came to study in a city – Sydney – that it was consumed and obsessed with desires I can only now begin to appreciate are toxic.

The moment I realised the nature of our desire for wealth, power and status, I began to see their global and personal impact. I felt overwhelming dismay and sadness. Both for the past, how people have treated each other, and for the world … but also a deep concern for the future.

It doesn't look like we will be containing the desire for wealth, power and status anytime soon. What would likely happen if they weren't? More exploitation and oppression? More pillaging of nature? Continued inequality and suffering globally at the hands of a few? We had reached a crossroads. These three toxic desires also threatened irreversible climate change and global nuclear war.

Just three basic human desires, born out of farming and unrecognised, had not only disconnected us from nature's healing and balancing qualities. They hadn't just detached us from being able to connect with our hearts and The All. Now they threatened all life in this blue and fragile world. The future didn't look rosy.

Okay, so what to do?

History has shown what has yet to work. Past religions and beliefs haven't contained our desire for wealth, power and status. On the contrary, some have probably empowered them – as mentioned earlier. Political systems haven't been able to restrict their destructive and unbalancing tendencies, and we can't expect them to. Preaching love hasn't made an impact either in over two thousand years. So, what then?

We can find a possible answer by realising what initially drove these three desires. What was the desire for wealth, power and status there to do? Ultimately, to help us feel safe and more secure. Since we know nature helped us feel safe and secure among each other in close tribal groups, some options come to mind.

Does this mean we must return to our nomadic tribal ways? No, it doesn't.

But perhaps friendship offers promise.

What if we all learned the practical reasons why friendship should be a priority in our life ahead of accumulating wealth, power and status? It would mean more social connection. It would mean more listening and respect. It would mean more caring and sharing. Market economies can still flourish. We can still make profits, but we would quickly recognise the poisonous extremes of wealth as signs of a more profound, more toxic dis-ease.

Progress, I knew, would need to be made in steps. So my next step was to write about the three desires and how we can reconnect using friendship. Hence the book, *The Friendship Key to Lasting Peace, United Communities, Stronger Relationships, Equality and a Better Job!*

Would friendship alone contain the three toxic desires that had become so entrenched? Probably not, but it would be a beginning. One thing was sure: unless we contained the desire for wealth, power and status, women would have to continue to fight for the respect they deserve as bringers of life and carers of our children and most vulnerable. Until our three poisonous desires were caged, we could expect to continue struggling to find peace, a balanced, harmonious world and lasting personal satisfaction.

Thankfully, nature and The All have also given us a way out. The ability to understand and correct our weaknesses and vulnerabilities – conscious thought, awareness and understanding. The ability to truly understand our heartfelt desires, feelings and their impact on each other and everything else.

Once I had written about friendship and the three malicious desires of greed, my attention gradually turned to trying to help us better master our fears.

As I looked around globally and at the many clients presenting with anxiety at our practice, I saw a need to share a simple way to resolve fears based on the approaches I used leading up to my connection with The All. I knew if we were ever to have a balanced and peaceful world, we also needed to be able to master our fears. Thankfully, there are easy skills that can help us accomplish this. Understanding and resolving fear would also teach critical introductory steps of communicating with feelings – learning their language and changing or transforming them. Finally, it would bring us closer to connection with The All itself.

CHAPTER 9

MASTERING FEAR AND COMMUNICATING WITH FEELINGS

Grey curtain-covered cubicles lined the corridor to my right and left. If I walked straight ahead to my left, at the end of the booths would be another small two rooms with sliding doors and opposite them plastic seating – for acute minor emergencies such as stitches. Behind me, at the corridor's end, a common staff room with tables linked together to form one large desk was where we wrote our notes – no computers then. The next door opened to the director's office, a very knowledgeable, patient, kindly chap with a well-worn, crinkled face, who would eventually shyly earn an Order of Australia Medal and Senior Australian of the Year in 2016 – Dr Gordian Fulde. Yet, despite all the great support, I still found working in Sydney's St Vincent's Emergency so stressful I would often get stomach pains, at times so severe I almost called in sick.

Fear can present in many ways, from trembling, poor sleep, agitation, restlessness, nightmares, dry mouth, sweaty palms, and tingling in toes, fingers and lips to total freezing-like paralysis and involuntary diarrhoea such as what the WW2 bomber pilots had written about. I can barely imagine the fear involved for these young pilots and crew, especially as a recruit, with flack exploding around you, never knowing if the next one would kill you. For me, fear presented in a much milder way. As an intern, with little experience in a hectic teaching hospital with so few beds that we regularly had patients laying on mattresses in the corridor, it was stomach pains. For a moment, I wondered if I was getting an ulcer. Then, during other rotations outside of Emergency, I noticed the fear reduced.

Mastering fear

Fear, uncontrolled, can restrict and dominate our lives. When fear gets so bad that it affects our ability to function, such as not being able to work, do our shopping or meet with other people, we give fear the added title of being a disorder, such as suffering from an anxiety disorder. Other fear-associated disorders include phobias, panic attacks, agoraphobia, obsessive-compulsive disorder (OCD), and post-traumatic stress disorder (PTSD). We regard anxiety-related disorders as some of the most commonly recognised mental illnesses. Uncontrolled fear can trigger hopelessness – no escape from its cage.

On a personal level, uncontrolled fears are a tragic, horrific curse. At a social level, rampant fears can be devastating.

When I realised the potentially destructive effects of our desire for wealth, power and status, I failed to fully appreciate how much these malicious drives were being fuelled by fear. For instance, these three nasty desires are fuelled by the fear of not having enough, the terror of losing our advantage, living among the disadvantaged, and being open to abuse and oppression. What hope do we have of ever conquering the need to build empires, go to war, pillage nature and subjugate other people if we don't learn to conquer and master fear?

The privileged, driven by greed, will always create imbalance, pain and unnecessary struggle while controlled by fear and using fear to control others. Learning to overcome our fears, I soon realised, wasn't just beneficial to those of us unfortunate enough to suffer fear as a mental illness; it could also play a critical role in the future of us all.

Mind you, there is another powerful and personal reason to consider better understanding and mastering fear. By conquering fear, we set the scene to know and feel what is deep within our hearts and beyond without restriction. We will discuss the importance of mastering fear and how it allows us to connect with The All later.

It seems fear is the key: without making it our ally and learning to master it, all our hopes for a truly fulfilling, balanced, harmonious, sustainable way of life are impossible to achieve.

So, how do we master fear?

Many of you who suffer from anxiety may already know how to calm yourself by breathing, exercising regularly, meditating to calm your mind, and using mindfulness techniques to bring your mind into the calm of the now. Some of you who suffer from past traumas may have tried proven psychological therapies such as Cognitive Behavioural Therapy (CBT) and Eye Movement and Desensitisation and Reprocessing (EMDR). These are all worthy treatments and skills. But many of us fail to learn how to deal with and resolve some of the most troubling fears – worst-case scenarios, the terrible things we worry might happen.

How many of your fears are worrying about possibilities in your future?

The key I eventually found to help us all more easily master fear was to explain how our memories work.

How do memories and fears work?

Memories play a pivotal role in determining what we do. We use our memories to guide our actions. For example, if you have learned to drive a car, you know what to do when you get in, how to move the car about, and, preferably, how not to crash. Our brain is good at using memories and refining them, often through practice, so we become more effective and efficient.

But our brain is also made to survive in the natural world. It can come across scenarios it has no memory to tap into to be reassured it will be okay and survive. So, nature also created our brain to make us overreact the first time we encounter the unfamiliar to increase the chance of survival by making us stronger, faster and able to think more quickly. We know that reaction as a fear response. So, nature decided it's better to overreact the first time and survive than under-react and die – it's hard to create new memories later if we are dead.

Every time we encounter the unfamiliar, we can expect to feel afraid – fear is normal and a great way to keep us alive.

Fear, no matter how annoying, is on our side.

However, lurking in the background, our brain also considers the future.

Earlier, we learned that our brain constantly runs simulations about what might happen – simulating possible futures. It is doing the same with fear. If our brain creates scenarios that threaten to take away what we cherish and have an emotional connection to – threatening our basic human needs – then we feel fear. And our brain will keep triggering the fear of that nasty scenario until we give it what it wants.

What *does* our brain want to make fear of catastrophes of the future go away? Mainly just one of two things: a plan or acceptance.

Our brain wants a memory – nerve connections – that indicates we will be okay – what we know as a plan. Or to know there is nothing we can do that will make a difference – what we know as acceptance.

Ultimately, our brain wants a plan or acceptance to resolve most of our fears. But, unfortunately, our brain keeps bothering us with feelings of fear; until we give it the future memory it needs to know that it will be okay. We will consider a few ways we can create such positive future memories in a moment.

It soon became apparent that by using these simple understandings of fear we can conquer the worst of fears, even the fears of getting cancer and dying. How many of us are afraid to die or get a terminal illness?

In my journey to connect with The All, you may recall that I had to conquer my worst fears. So how did I do it? First, I faced them. Then I called their bluff. Finally, I let them give me their best shot, and they – unexpectedly at the time – passed through me and faded away. This approach formed the foundations for my last book, *Taming Fear in the Age of Covid*. Another recommended technique from the book involved holding the fear and asking it what it wants for it to go away. I have used this technique so many times in different ways I often don't realise I'm doing it anymore. What I didn't more fully appreciate until I finished the fear book was that what I'd been teaching was the beginnings of how to communicate with feelings – a skill I acquired out of necessity as I climbed my internal mountain in my mid-twenties.

Ultimately, fear, in its most basic sense, is a feeling. We can learn to communicate with fears to help understand them and make them disappear. This ability to communicate with fear is a skill we can also begin to apply to master and communicate with feelings.

Communicate with feelings – the beginning

Imagine an old guy in a massive library littered with aisle after aisle of books. We ask the affable chap if he could please find information on tigers. 'Are you sure?' he asks, his eyebrow raised, wrinkling his already withered forehead. 'Oh, yes, tigers, please.' He is off, shuffling along. Minutes, maybe hours pass, then he returns with a fine book on tigers. By now, we want to know about donkeys; we no longer need to learn about tigers. 'Ah, could you get me a book about donkeys? I really want to know about donkeys.' With a sigh of disappointment, 'Are you sure?' he asks. 'Oh, yes, donkeys.' He clutches the book he has to his chest and shuffles off. Hours pass. He comes back with an excellent thick book. But so much time has passed, we now want to know about rabbits. After a while, the old chap takes longer and longer, taking the time to have a cup of tea. Why should he even bother getting the book for us when we want something else by the time he gives it to us? We never give proper attention to what he has to show us.

It is similar to our minds. We often have questions, like what is life about, what is my place among all things, or what am I afraid of and why? We ask the question once, put it to our mind, then, as life goes on, we are distracted and feel the urge to know about something else. We never persevere enough to get the answers that our minds can provide. We don't persist.

That was the key to finding answers and getting past obstructions on my inner journey; I would persist. I remembered where I had left off and repeatedly asked the same question. To my surprise, I always received a helpful answer – eventually. If it wasn't the complete answer, it was often insight into a new way to consider the problem or a new path. Persistence was vital to making headway.

From persisting, I quickly learned that behind every question I was asking and the answer I was searching for were underlying scenarios. The scenarios showed me how things connected and worked. For instance, I once asked whether our minds can think instantly. As I held the question, I could see scenarios and images of my mind running at different rates. For example, I could think quickly when being logical and living life day-to-day – but I did not think instantly. But thinking with feelings and exploring them, I found, meant my mind was reacting more slowly. I then remembered some of my physiology and the role of adrenaline – epinephrine – during a fear response. Like all chemicals in our body, adrenalin takes time to build up and be released. It takes longer for our bodies to break it down. Hence, fear won't be instant, but once it is there, it can take longer to go away than we might like. Good to know if we have a panic attack, we can't expect it to settle instantly.

The answer to my question, thoughts might come and go rapidly, but feelings tend to ebb and flow at slower rates. Thoughts were not instant.

After my transcendent experience, my lifetime of accumulated fears didn't just magically disappear. They were still triggering me – especially fears from my childhood. I knew I needed to resolve them to find a greater sense of peace and explore more of what life had to offer. The difference now was I also had skills to use from my internal journey and the ability to see life from a perspective that made it easier to understand – the memory of The All.

The memory of The All experience allowed me to see myself as a being, trained to be who he was by life events and experiences. It allowed me to begin to see what moulded me. I am still working on comprehensively understanding the many influences that led me to react and feel as I am – that created my persona. But knowing The All meant I could realise all these events and reactions weren't me as a whole; they were just a part of me – they didn't define me or continue to define me unless I let them. It was similar with the fears I had accumulated; they did not define me unless I allowed them to because I had a way to rewrite them – to resolve them for good.

Knowing that feelings didn't define me – they were mostly a reaction to many life circumstances – took the pressure off. It eliminated critical self-judgement – why blame me for what wasn't my fault? It allowed me to explore feelings – including fears – more freely.

How do we connect with and rewrite fears?

If a fear arose, such as being alone or an outcast, I could hold it, keep it in my presence and preferably make it stronger. Then I would ask, where did you come from? I held the fear and the question, and soon memories appeared of actual events of my past. I had already learned to see beyond what I wanted or needed to believe – to find a sense of truth. I found the events and scenarios that had the associated specific feeling of that fear. I could then explore those events and see if I would feel differently with a few changes in how I considered the event. It worked. I did.

For instance, being ostracised and bashed up was still a social fear. As I explored the fear and asked what made these guys want to bash me, I began to see the whole event with different eyes. For example, would the boys have treated me like this if the boys' parents had been more compassionate and understanding? No, probably not. Would

I have been ostracised if my father had been better at making friends and had taught me those skills? Probably not. Was the incident my fault? No. Was there anything I could have done as this young boy that would have made a difference? No. With these realisations, I found the peace of acceptance and a better understanding of people's motives – a plan. I had rewritten and resolved this fear.

As I explored fears more, I quickly learned that each fear feels slightly different – its feeling is unique. It reminds me of the old library cards with numbers that would allow you to find a book. The number on the card was unique, and at the other end was a specific book. Fears, I found, were similar. Behind each feeling of fear was a unique scenario or set of scenarios or events. Every fear held a scenario, either a memory of the past or a memory of what hasn't happened yet – a simulation. And every scenario could be understood, rewritten and resolved.

This realisation was a breakthrough in understanding fear and unlocking the secrets of feelings.

There were many tricks or skills to learn to make communicating with fears and mastering them easier. Eventually, I devised a set of simple and safe steps so we can more easily explore and befriend our fears – even the worst-case scenarios. I share these steps in *Taming Fear in the Age of Covid*.

Like learning how to communicate with fear, we can learn to communicate with feelings. But, learning to explore the most subtle feelings, I realised we have access to far more of the human experience than we are familiar with.

In the next chapter, we will begin by learning how to make sense of feelings in a way that promotes wisdom. Then, we will learn the value of searching inside feelings we often avoid – our darker side or shadows often hold the most valuable understandings. After that, we will know to ground ourselves by increasing our sense of self so we don't get lost in chaos and uncertainty. With so many people's varied opinions, how are we supposed to know what to believe? A non-selfish, well-grounded, positive sense of genuine self can be an invaluable guide.

Finally, we will learn how to gain profound insight into our feelings, actions and experiences through developing empathy and building a greater understanding of feelings through theorising for ourselves. That way, we don't have to learn about how feelings work from others, such as scientists or psychologists, but by learning to examine feelings critically and unlock their secrets from within.

In chapter 11, we will learn how we can use connecting with feelings to begin to discover the deepest secrets of perhaps one of the most perplexing and diverse feelings of all – romantic love.

CHAPTER 10

FEELINGS – WISDOM, GROUNDING AND SELF-DISCOVERY

Peering through the almost clear glass of my loungeroom windows, vague balls of fluffy white merged into ever-changing shapes of clouds spanning my vision. The vista layered before me; closer were palm fronds dancing in the breeze, to their left spires of swaying bamboo. Beyond them, not a kilometre away, the occasional crow found a branch in a cluster of trees and then departed. Much further distant, a long hill blanketed by trees folded slightly to its right, giving the illusion of three hills blending into one. It was a break from writing this book. For less than an hour, I meditated as I stared at the scene before me, contemplating how the restricted views and behaviours of others in my past still impacted my persona, able to peer into the feelings and circumstances behind them and relate them to the now. Then, with a gentle sigh, I realised something new I hadn't noticed before. Behind the sigh represented a greater sense of inner peace and knowing.

Understanding, appreciating and using feelings to improve our lives is not a one-off achievement but an ongoing process. We are not perfect; fully realising our humanity and its potential will always be a path of refinement. Even the path to discovering on earth the harmony, balance and realisation of our place and fulfilling the essence of The All's potential instilled within us – to realise the fullness of our human perspective – will always be ongoing. For me, the adage is true; the more we know, the more we realise we don't have a clue – there is so much to learn and embrace if we are open to considering it.

We are about to learn to use feelings to help us unlock some of the mysteries of our humanity and beyond. By using feelings in different ways, as we shall soon see, we will also be better able to appreciate the potential for deep insight that feelings offer and their practical application towards engaging positive change.

We will use four simple steps, beginning by using feelings as a vehicle for increased personal wisdom – to become functional, more self-aware human beings. Then, we will understand the importance of seeing into our shadows and using them as a source of greater knowledge and growth. Thirdly, we will learn how to use feelings to ground ourselves by creating solid foundations of genuine self, giving us confidence we are on the right path of self-realisation and knowing. Finally, we will learn how to use feelings as a tool of ongoing discovery to explore within ourselves and beyond, every step bringing us closer to realising The All and a more profound, fulfilling human experience.

Practically, we will learn steps to understand, explore and master any feeling we choose. Don't like how you feel? We will now have the tools to know why we feel this way and how to change it. Feelings don't make sense? Learn what they are about and what they want from us. If you want a closer and more intimate connection with The

All – a purer personal experience of God – we will learn ways to make it easier to achieve within a lifetime.

We are not talking about using science to explain how we feel by describing biology and behavioural approaches; we are talking about us making practical sense of feelings and mastering them ourselves on the inside – no books required. We won't need anyone to tell us how it is. Instead, we will learn how to find answers we can trust.

We are about to journey into our hearts and let them reveal their true and wondrous nature.

Let us begin to make sense of feelings by using them to increase our wisdom.

Step 1. The golden question as a path to wisdom

I will not debate what wisdom is or isn't as much as consider wisdom as learning what works, through experience and insight. For example, repeatedly making the same mistakes isn't wise. Doing things that are counter to our long-term interests isn't wise either. On the other hand, learning to be functional and fulfilled human beings able to live in balance with nature would be considered wise – it works better for us all in the long run.

Feelings, I learned, can be a fast track to wisdom. How?

Through asking one simple yet critical question …

What does the feeling want from me? With this simple question, we begin to link a feeling or feelings to actions. How this simple act increases wisdom and promotes self-awareness will become apparent shortly.

Take a moment. What do you feel right now? You don't have to put it into words; you don't need to. What do the feelings you are having now want from you? Do you feel the need to keep reading and learning? Do you need to make dinner, get a snack or drink water? Do you feel the need to pee?

Of course, not all feelings seem to want anything from us. For instance, some feelings can be rewards, such as pleasure after meeting up with a close friend. Pleasure can be seen as nature patting us on the back and saying: 'Please do more of that; it is a worthwhile thing.'

Similarly, feelings of displeasure or emotional pain indicate we should do something different – to make the pain disappear.

Ultimately, we can still link every feeling as wanting something from us.

As we have seen, feelings can have infinite variations and ebb and flow. So one of the fastest ways to make sense of them is to be practical with them from the start.

Are you still having trouble working out what your feeling wants from you? We can make it easier by asking the following two questions in addition:

Do I feel fear?

Do I feel I want something?

You may remember, soon after my experience with The All, I tried to make sense of feelings and their infinite variations. Ultimately, I broke feelings into two main groups: fears and desires. No matter what is happening to us, whether we cut our arm, poke a needle in our finger or haven't drunk any water in over a day, we will still have a combination of fear and desire within us manifesting in some way. The fear may be so quiet we don't notice it, and we may only notice what we want – give me a drink now, please. But, on the other hand, the fear may be so great we don't notice our desires – it is time to step away from the oncoming car; the drink can wait. Or we can have a combination of both fear and desire, such as when we feel excitement.

Have you ever felt excited? What did you feel like knowing you were about to do something naughty and it would feel good, too? Did you feel the tingles of anticipation and excitement? I know I have. Like feeling excited, many feelings can be a combination of fear and desire.

Remember, our fears can be so mild they barely keep us awake. Then, they can rise to agitation, discomfort, nervousness and anxiety. Finally, they can peak at total paralysing terror. At any point, we feel fear somewhere along its spectrum. Sit quietly for a moment – no distractions – and peer into your feeling. Can you notice any suggestions of fear within that feeling? It's okay if you don't.

Similarly, desires can present as spectrums from mildly hungry, for instance, to ravenous hunger. But don't forget, as mentioned a moment ago, the feelings associated with desires also present as pleasure and displeasure.

As you notice your feelings now, perhaps you see little fear or desire but feel content.

What is contentment, and where does it fall into the spectrums of fear and desire? What do feelings of contentment want from us?

Contentment wants very little, if anything. Feeling content means there are no significant fears to make us want to act on them and no important desires to pursue – there are no drives to do much at all. Hence, we feel calm and at peace. Contentment is excellent and worth working towards.

Try the following exercise for a week to help apply our new understanding of feelings. Five times a day, ask yourself how you feel and what the feeling wants from you. Set your alarm to remind you if you wish. Then ask, is your feeling linked to fear, desire or both? You don't have to answer these fears or desires yet; just be aware they are there for now.

With just a simple practice, we can become very feeling aware – self-aware. The more we practice this simple exercise, the more self-aware we become.

With repetition, you may notice you have many combinations of feelings at any one time and that they can quickly change – this is normal. Focus on what you feel now when you ask the question.

Take your time. Get used to recognising your feelings, whether they relate to fear, desire or both, and what they might want from you. Every time you practise this, you are teaching your mind there is a connection between what you feel and what you do in the world. You are linking the vastness, depth and subtleness of each unique feeling to physical events and actions. No words are needed. Developing this practical connection is a significant step in a journey to self-awareness and exploring what is beyond. It is hard to notice what we can feel beyond us if we can't even see what we feel here and now.

We can take this awareness and learning to another level of practical insight and self-understanding. Are you ready?

Once you recognise your fear and desire, you can ask them more specifically what they want to be satisfied or resolved.

As we have seen, for fears to exist, our brain is running a simulation, a set of scenarios it wants us to act upon. Now consider the fear you can recognise and ask it what it wants you to do for the fear to go away. Ask it. If you struggle to find the answers, try the gentle stepwise approach outlined in *Taming Fear in the Age of Covid*.

Mastering fear, by definition, requires understanding what feelings want from us and being able to answer them. Do you notice any fears lurking that want something from you, in your family life, work or socially, for instance? Are you worried about the state of world affairs? Great, now work to resolve these fears, and you will understand the feelings of fear or anxiety.

We can use a similar approach with the feelings of desire and the experience of pleasure and displeasure that go with them. In this case, we can use the BOS Model to help us better understand what the desires want from us.

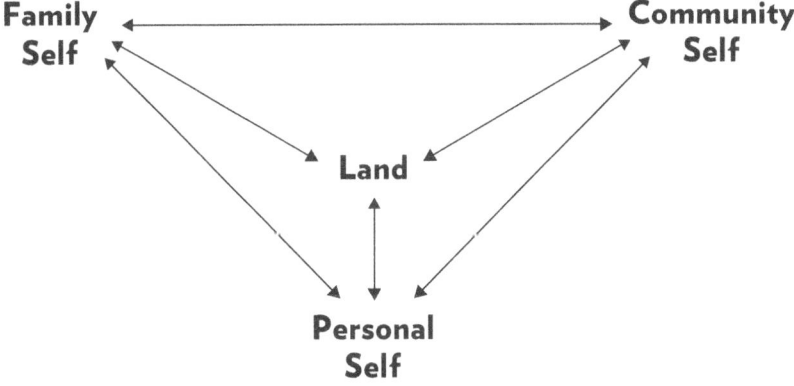

In many ways, we can liken the BOS Model to a Rosetta Stone to the heart. Just as the Rosetta Stone, dating back to 196 BC, gave modern linguists an unprecedented ability to read and interpret unreadable Egyptian hieroglyphs, the BOS Model also offers a practical means to make sense of our seemingly innumerable desires. It helps us analyse – and translate – feelings of craving, wanting, pleasure and displeasure into how they affect our actions and what we can do to gain fulfilment. Each of the human essences described in the BOS Model indicates what desires seek from us to find satisfaction, pleasure and contentment. The BOS Model can be a guide out of misery, but in a balanced, sustainable way.

Let us see what might fit into each category within the BOS Model, then look at how you might satisfy or fulfil them. Consider the following examples.

For instance, is your body crying out for better care? Are you feeling regularly tired, sore or in physical discomfort? Are you as fit as you know you should be? Do you seek time alone to be in nature or listen to your heart? Any feelings related to maintaining your health and well-being and connecting with your heart and nature are feelings you can recognise as part of your Personal Self.

Are you spending enough time with the children? Are you spending enough quality time with your partner to maintain a profoundly satisfying relationship? Are you seeking a romantic relationship and all the pleasures that can go with it? Any feelings that drive you to form romantic relationships and care for and maintain families are examples of desires you can recognise as part of the Family Self. We will explore the nature of feelings and desires of romantic love within the Family Self in greater detail soon.

Do you feel alone, worthless or that you are not making enough of a difference in life? Are you feeling different, isolated, unsafe or insecure? Do you crave to have your contribution recognised, valued and appreciated by others, such as through study or work? Suppose you have desires or feelings related to how you get on with others and wanting to be part of bigger supportive groups or communities such as a business, political organisation, religion or local social group. In that case, you can recognise them as part of the Community Self.

Consider how you feel now. What are your most dominant feelings – the most obvious? If you had to put these feelings into one of the categories of the BOS Model, then which would it be? If unsure, you might like to read about the different categories in greater detail in my book *A Balance of Self* to make it easier.

Sometimes it gives greater clarity to write your answers down. Try it.

My desire/feeling is primarily from the human essence of: *(circle one)*

a/ Personal Self
b/ Family Self
c/ Community Self

My fear is:

Practice looking at what your feelings want from you in the real world, what they want you to do. For example, do they want you to satisfy a desire, avoid what might harm you, seek a plan of action, or know there is nothing you do that will make a difference? Do your feelings want to reward you, so you do something again or drive you to change, so you don't feel so miserable? Over time as you practice these simple exercises, your feelings will begin to make much greater sense. They will also clarify what you need to do to feel more satisfied and fulfilled, such as work at increasing your Personal, Family or Community Self and their aspects.

You may have noticed that not a single emotion has been named. It hasn't been necessary. Understanding feelings in terms of what they want us to do can save us from trying to find words we know will never fully explain what we feel. We can develop a profound understanding of feelings without using many, if any, words.

The more we understand what our feelings want from us, the more we know the fundamentals of being a balanced and functional human being. By only asking a few simple questions, we offer to immeasurably increase our understanding of what we feel and why. Along the way, we automatically become wiser as we begin to see what works and what doesn't.

Step 2. Flashlight in the dark

One of the biggest threats to developing a functional insight into feelings is not looking at and resolving the feelings that trouble us the most. These could be feelings of childhood abandonment, anger to the point of uncontrolled rage, feelings of severe guilt, worthlessness, hate, being different, alone, and unloved or unlovable. We all carry what many call our 'shadow' – the dark part of us we don't like and which works against us. The temptation is to avoid the dark and keep away from our shadow. Yet, we can find our most extraordinary positive insights and wisdom within the shadow's feelings. Most of what I have learned about our nature, what satisfies us, and the breadth and depth of the human experience has often come from exploring and bringing light to my pains and discomforts.

Does peering into our shadow mean we support and empower all that is negative inside us? Not at all. Imagine a dark room with only a candle giving a glow of comforting light. If we only focus on getting closer to the light, won't the shadows grow more prominent and darker behind us? We need to light more candles in the shadows, or preferably, shine a torch into the darkness, so it no longer influences us. The more we avoid whatever bothers us, the more it takes control. Fear is a classic example.

I had a client in his early seventies who was so afraid his very mild prostate cancer would kill him that he became so engrossed in his grief that he stopped living. He stopped playing with his grandchild who he adored, meeting his good friends, going fishing, bowling – living life. His fear of death and that cancer would end him ahead of schedule – he had at least another fifteen years to go – controlled him and took what remaining joy of life he could have still had away. Thankfully, we could delve into the sorrow and change his perspective to allay his fears. But, unfortunately, fears unfaced and unresolved, as alluded to earlier, can easily restrict our life and control us.

Not only can our shadows control us they can also seriously harm us. Addictions are a typical example. Addictions to drugs, alcohol, sex, adrenalin, social media, pornography – you name it – will ultimately be driven by one or more basic human needs not being met. We are chasing the scream, a loud enough emotional noise – experience – that will drown out our discomfort. In the process, we can destroy our bodies, relationships, careers and friendships – anything to avoid the pain in the shadows.

We can also deny, avoid, emotionally detach and seek salvation to cope with the darkness within.

Denying we have a problem can quickly make us feel better – in the short term. But it doesn't make our problem go away. Many of us use denial to help us manage our emotional pains. Our relationship is fine; I don't see a problem, even though you argue daily and barely enjoy each other's company. The relationship isn't okay, and denial won't help restore it.

When negative emotions get too much, we can always avoid what seems to trigger them, like certain people, gatherings, work, TV shows and going outside. However, suppose we take avoidance too far. In that case, we are soon trapped in a cage around us more robust than any metal and perhaps more restrictive.

Or you can do what I had been taught – emotionally detach. Again, the brain has an excellent safety mechanism. If emotions get too much, it shuts them down by detaching us, as if we aren't in the body feeling them anymore. This experience is well described during sexual assaults where the victim may view the assault from a distance – outside their body – or as if it was happening to someone else. Detach us enough, and soon we cannot emotionally feel pleasure or joy in any deep and present sense. While growing up, my dreams and desires were squashed so often that I protected myself by not feeling much at all.

To cope with the emotional discomfort and distress, we can also seek salvation, either a person such as a doctor or a therapist who will cure us or some all-powerful supernatural goodness that will protect and save us. However, seeking salvation without working to resolve what lies in the shadows is like drinking from a poisoned chalice. It immediately disempowers us, so we never learn to resolve the issues for ourselves. Seeking a saviour also opens us to being manipulated and controlled by unsavoury sorts. Seeking salvation doesn't resolve the darkness; it can often take us deeper.

Can we use feelings to help us counter our negative traits and rid us of so much internal pain and suffering? Yes, we can, and we can begin with a torch of truth and honesty. We start by getting brutally honest with ourselves.

Ultimately, deep down, we know when we are lying to ourselves. If we have doubts, we use the technique I learned on my internal quest – to continue searching for truth rather than what makes us feel good.

Be open to being wrong and making mistakes. Be open to discovering and facing your fears and pains. Allow space for what lurks in your shadow and hold them – make space for the worst feelings – no critical judgement. Just hold the space with them and let them be there. Then, remind us that we do our best according to what has happened to us and what others have taught us – we did our best in the circumstances.

Walking into the dark is a natural and powerful part of positive transformation. To conquer the shadow allows us to be open to more feelings and experiences – it frees our hearts. In many ways, our inner darkness is like an anchor holding us back from living our potential as a person and connecting beyond ourselves.

Once we're in the dark and seeing its truth, what do we do?

We ask the questions in step one – we find out what these feelings want of us and answer them in a more functional and less harmful way. Then, if we need to, we rewrite our past; as I mentioned, I am still doing it. Finally, if we need professional help to do this, we seek it – there is no shame in seeking help from those experienced to get us out of the shadows.

Step 3. Build strong foundations of self

Inside each of us waiting to awaken and realise is the essence of humanity that The All instilled, so we can be fulfilled human beings in balance and harmony with nature. Our greatest, most helpful truth is within, locked within feelings we can all learn to access. If we hope to make sense of feelings honestly, we need to be able to access their truth, their purer form. We need to feel grounded and build strong foundations that feel true.

Where inside us is this key to our honest, balanced humanity? Deep within our Personal Self – a part of us that is far less corrupted by the toxic effects of others.

Before I began my internal journey in isolation, I asked myself a critical question. Suppose our society – and humanity in general – has lost its way and no longer knows what works. Where can I look to find a better direction? The answer was obvious: inside me, but I would need to look inside in a way that disregarded anything others had shown me and I'd been taught or learned – beyond the corruption. Once I succeeded and found a source of insight untainted by others – a connection with The All – I was reminded of the same question when I created the BOS model. I was reminded again of the question when I realised the severely damaging effects of our uncontrolled desire for wealth, power and status. Can we trust the knowledge and wisdom of such a broken system and its representatives? We need another source to help us rediscover our true hearts. In practical terms, we find it within a robust Personal Self.

Peer inside, and we find a tribal person with specific tribal needs – our heart is tribal (see page 75). How can we realise this tribal person and bring them contentment? We could try finding a connection with native tribes. But what if the corruption of modern ways has also contaminated their ways? Or we could, as I learned to do, redefine ourselves using nature.

We can increase our sense of Personal Self in many ways. Anything that draws us to hold onto feelings from within can help. For instance, the expression of feelings from within as art, sculpture, poetry, story, cooking, dancing and music all enhance our sense of Personal Self, so long as we don't do them to impress anyone and we express them for ourselves alone.

For example, when we write a story or poem for ourselves alone, or we make a meal we can indulge in without sharing; when we write a song and sing it simply because it makes us feel good, or dance because it connects us to the rhythm of our physical form; when we paint or sculpt an image that evokes a feeling we want to get out from within. Each act requires us to tap into a deeper part of our heart no one else can ever honestly know and let us be closer to a genuine part of us that is representative of our Personal Self – the unique us.

Try it; feel from within and express these feelings and inspirations in the outside world – let your heart come out and express it physically as if no one is watching, and no one ever needs to know. You can choose the medium. Talent or skill is irrelevant – develop your own. How deep are the feelings of inspiration? What do we need to get out? What honest part of us needs to emerge that we can grasp and see that is a genuine part of us?

Some of you may recognise that nothing we express in art will ever be entirely outside of the influence of others. That is true, but creative expression from within can be a tremendous start in the search for a genuine sense of self.

If we are to seek a purer source of connection with a more pristine essence beyond humanity's corruption, nature offers a brilliant source.

Increasing our Personal Self with nature offers us a different definition of ourselves and our place in the universe. Spending time in nature reminds us, as it did when I was inspired by meditating on the tree in my uni years, that we are more than part of a community. We are more than part of a family: son, daughter, mother, father, uncle, aunt or grandparent. We are also individuals in our own right with individual needs that are part of a greater whole. We are created to develop our relationship with The All – or purer realisation of God – and nurture a unique, honest, personal sacred connection.

By maintaining a purer untainted connection with nature, I discovered we could help ensure we realise our purer self as nature – The All – intended it to be.

As we have noted, unfortunately, communities tend to corrupt the purity of the connection we can develop with our more genuine selves. Still, if we recognise this degradation, we can use a strong sense of Personal Self to regain our bearings.

Will communities try to stop us from achieving this level of personal connection? Only the societies that don't value our individuality and connection beyond ourselves.

In an unstable society where people are oppressed and basic needs aren't met, individual thought and action – being true to our heart – is bound to be discouraged, perhaps outlawed. We, as self-aware individuals, threaten the status quo and greater instability. At the very least, such a dysfunctional society will remind us always to put the community and others first and listen to society ahead of us – to assimilate and obey. Hence, when we try to find a strong sense of self, we become labelled as selfish.

It makes sense why we use the selfish term so much today. To look after self in a society driven by the greedy desire for wealth, power and status means stepping over others to get to the top – being individualistic to the point of being self-absorbed. Self in such a society does equate to selfishness. But, as we noted earlier, enhancing Personal Self is different.

Enhancing the Personal Self is increasing connection and realising our deeper desires as tribal-inspired beings. If we are faithful to these desires, will we still want to help others, especially in their time of need?

Of course, we will want to. How is that selfish? It isn't.

Increasing Personal Self is not being selfish. Without a robust Personal Self, we lose the most profound emotional connection with others, including our neighbours, partners, children and nature. We lose connection with our purer, genuine, wiser self.

How can we use nature to increase our Personal Self?

Ideally, we need to immerse ourselves in it. We are more than just sightseeing or hiking from one place to the next. We need to allow ourselves to *feel* nature.

We can take inspiration from tribal cultures here. Imagine a spirit within every creature, blade of grass, tree, rock, mountain or hill. What would it notice? What might its desires be if it had any?

Let yourself be one of the trees around you. Can you sense the other trees? Try to see all in nature from the tree's unique point of view. What might it feel like to be them?

Feel, don't analyse. Instead, let your feelings explore what you can sense around you. Notice how being in this place among these spirits changes how you feel? What do the feelings of these spirits want of each other? What do these spirits want of us?

You recall earlier, we mentioned how Country has language (see page 57). If you want to increase your Personal Self, try learning to listen more to nature's language. What is it trying to teach you? Is your heart open enough to listen?

If you don't have access to nature, a local park, tree, plants or the sky will do. Reflect upon their spirits. Develop your emotional connection with it. Let it help to reveal how you honestly feel – your inner feelings.

There is a whole repository of honest feelings to help us realise the true nature of our hearts waiting for us to discover it – foundations that bring us closer to the true nature of The All inside us.

What do you think and feel independently of others?

Step 4. Power of empathy and inquiry

How do feelings work? Why do I feel this way? And how can we use feelings as a tool of inquiry and insight – to find answers?

We can take understanding feelings to the next level by taking on a receptive persona, learning a means of self-investigation and improving our empathy.

Other people can help teach us enormous amounts about feelings. After all, how many of our feelings exist due to our interactions with others? More than a few.

We will begin by developing a receptive persona to help us make sense of and use what we learn – a suitable vessel to put our new understanding in.

Build a receptive persona

I recall a client on a journey of self-discovery who would always – almost every moment of every day – try to notice what she felt and why. She'd learned to do this from reading and joining spiritually focused groups. Unfortunately, her mind was a shambles. She couldn't make sense of or use almost anything she noticed. The process left her emotionally disconnected from her true feelings, other people and the world; her mind was clouded with a fog of random details.

If we explore feelings alone, without grounding, it is easy to get lost. A simple way to ground us is to create a persona.

What do I mean by a persona?

It was a trick I learned as an intern – medical trainee – and as I was learning to become a medical specialist. I imagined I was already a specialist, and I visualised I could recall greatly detailed information and use it. I imagined already making sense of enormous amounts of data and applying it to patients. This visualisation offered my mind a framework, like branches of a tree, to organise my knowledge and add to it in a way I could use, rather than just another piece of knowledge to add to a pile of information. By imagining being a specialist, it was easier to start becoming one.

It is similar when trying to understand feelings. If we have a persona that already includes how the new awareness and knowledge feelings bring can be used and applied, then what we learn isn't just some excellent random insight. Now the experience has a slot or place in our mind to fit into – it has purpose and meaning. As a result, it is easier to use and make sense of.

What sort of receptive persona should I create? The following suggestions can help you decide and give you insight into what characteristics you would like your receptive persona to take:

- A mother or father who knows how feelings work so they can share and offer wisdom to their children, giving them a better, more satisfying life experience.
- A therapist of great wisdom and experience, able to integrate personal insights with socially accepted understandings and use them to help others live more fulfilling, less traumatic lives.

- A wise woman like those of ancient tribes who seeks to know feelings so she can pass on her insight by example with generations to come.
- A wise man like an ancient tribal elder seeking to understand feelings so they can help better guide and offer wise counsel to help others and improve their lives.
- A being sent here to help our world through a difficult transition, already aware of how we are all connected and trying to share wisdom to help integrate us into a universal, caring, supportive, peaceful whole.
- A person who already understands some of the greatest mysteries of being human, connected with and able to realise The All, also able to sense the beyond-infinite wish of wellness and fulfilment of all beings and seeking to make it a reality through a greater understanding of feelings.
- A modern-day shaman, a spiritual man or woman connecting with the beyond and its peace and wisdom to share and personify it here.

Whether the persona is real or not is irrelevant. Even the persona we have now is a construct; we can easily argue it isn't real, but it helps us get by in the world.

Is creating a persona faking it until we make it? It is, to an extent. For example, we dress the part and take on the persona of a businessman instead of a store assistant. In that case, we are more likely to fit the role and be accepted as a businessman when the opportunity arises, so long as we have done our homework, such as having the necessary qualifications. And because we already have a businessman persona, we are more ready and able to accept businessman-related approaches and ideas; we are more receptive and better able to use them.

There is no right or wrong persona. Choose what resonates with you, then stick with it – don't just keep randomly changing it. That would be like trying to build on shifting sands; it won't allow you the stability to build a sturdy understanding of the feelings around it.

The next step is to build, test and evolve your theories.

A method of self-inquiry

Our aim is simple: to teach ourselves to learn and develop new ideas and insights into ourselves and others without relying on almost anything from traditional learning, such as books.

In other words, creating a method of learning that is based primarily on our own experiences – yet, in a critical way, that continues to develop so we don't get caught up believing whatever we want that isn't very realistic and ultimately doesn't work. Once we have our own ideas, we can compare them with what others have found or discovered and see where we are, compared to them. Understanding what we think and feel about feelings should come first, then we compare.

The approach I like to use to ensure I develop my ideas based on my experience and perspective is to imagine everyone is wrong. Try it. Imagine everyone is wrong about feelings, the ideas might sound okay, but ultimately, they are not true, even what you read in this book. Then it is time to see what ideas and possibilities you come up with. Your insights and approaches may be very different. Great. Evolve the ideas and see where they go. This understanding is your wisdom that you are growing true to your heart, not someone else's.

Why is it important not to listen to others here?

We are not trying to evolve a truth everyone can agree on – an absolute truth – we are trying to get you to realise and develop your personal truth more fully first. You cannot connect beyond yourself unless you evolve true to yourself in a purer sense, true to your heart, insights and experiences.

How do we evolve our ideas about feelings? First, we develop a theory or hypothesis; then, we see if we are right. Consider the following example.

Feel, wonder, see

Have you ever felt angry, perhaps even total rage? The pressure builds, the agitation grows, and it can get to the point where you explode and can then do regrettable physical damage such as hitting an object or person. Anger is a normal feeling. But what is the nature of anger?

I used to be easily triggered by anger for years. Thankfully, I was also taught not to act on it, so I rarely took it out on others or physical objects – like punching a wall or striking someone. However, I'm not too fond of anger; I didn't want to be angry, so I decided to peer inside my anger to understand it.

I began by wondering where did anger come from? In other words, when did it first become prominent in my life? I'd already learned one of the fastest ways to understand many feelings is to know when they started – what triggered them. After that one incident, the feeling can be learned behaviour – becoming like a habit. So, I put the question to my heart and mind; I persisted, and images finally appeared of my childhood, mainly relating to my father.

I soon recalled my father used to be an angry man and would quickly take out his anger on anyone in the family around him. Suddenly, I remembered being angry with my mother for not doing things the way my father wanted and making him upset. Once he was angry, I was often terrified.

Then I wondered, how much anger is driven by fear? So I examined as many situations as possible of past anger experiences and when it was triggered in the present. Could I feel fear within them? Yes, I could. But were there times I felt no fear and still felt anger? I found them too.

I also noted I became angry when I was frustrated – things didn't go as I wanted, usually after many things not going to plan, one after the other. I would get very angry when it seemed like I was fighting against the world. A clear example for me was when I was training Zoe – the sheepdog – and things weren't going well – thankfully, that was rare.

Did fear and frustration account for all my experiences of feeling anger? I searched within. I also kept an eye out whenever I had the slightest anger and would look inside to see if there was more there than fear, frustration or both. It seemed just fear and frustration fuelled virtually all my anger.

Out of this realisation, I came to ask myself, when I was angry, what was I afraid of? Was it getting in trouble? Was it still a fear of my father's response? I would ask, search for the truth and images would appear, telling me what I feared. Once I knew the fear and resolved it, the anger reduced to the point of only ever being mild and occasional. For example, my anger at being late for an appointment or to meet someone – a trait I learned from the anger of my father – virtually disappeared.

Knowing fear and frustration triggered anger, I could also predict my anger would most likely appear when I was afraid, such as when

I was under stress or falling behind. Feeling the pressure reminded me to calm myself.

Did I read up on anger to try to understand it? No. Instead, I took simple steps. Steps we can apply to better understanding almost any feeling.

Firstly, I began by recognising a feeling I wanted to understand; in this example, the feeling was anger. I then sought to identify what was lying beneath the feeling. The next step was to look for a possible trigger from the past of the underlying feeling (in this example, fear), not the feeling initially explored (in this example, anger). I did find fear as a trigger. I then hypothesised that fear was primarily driving my anger. After that, I looked for evidence to prove I was right. I looked into my past experiences of anger for proof – was the feeling of fear always present within anger? It seemed I was right most of the time, but not always. It appeared there were times there was no fear involved at all.

I began the steps just outlined again. This time, I looked for possible triggers of frustration resulting in anger. I found a possible link. I hypothesised that frustration was also a trigger for anger. I looked into the memories of anger that couldn't be explained as being triggered or driven by fear and found all the remaining seemed to be triggered by frustration. I better understood a feeling (in this case, anger) and hadn't learned any of it from a book.

Later, as a doctor, I had the privilege to have others share their experiences. I wondered how many of my clients complaining of anger had also become angry out of fear or frustration. I couldn't find evidence of anger that wasn't, to some extent, driven by fear, frustration or both.

Does that mean my theory is correct? Most, if not all, anger is driven by fear – often taught – and frustration. No. But so long as I keep an open mind to other possibilities, my theories can develop and become more valuable – closer to some form of absolute truth.

Do I need to know the absolute truth of anger to master it? No. As you just noticed, once I understood what triggered anger in my life, I now had experiences I could rewrite, such as resolving my fears of past traumas relating to my father that often fuelled my rage or anger.

But what if I develop these theories and they are ultimately wrong?

Let them be wrong. Every theory we ever come up with will ultimately be wrong since, as we noted earlier, we don't see everything – our ideas will always be incomplete. But in developing our personal truth, it doesn't matter if we are wrong, so long as we know this is our best right now. And so long as our truth is workable, can improve our lives and help us restore balance, who cares if we or others eventually say it is wrong? It doesn't matter in the long run.

Does this method of self-learning mean I shouldn't be open to what others may say about feelings and their own experiences? No. We must listen and try to understand what others have experienced and their ideas. But the big mistake would be giving up and replacing our developing ideas with theirs. Modify your ideas instead.

You are developing your understanding of feelings. Take in whatever information is available and then draw your conclusions and ideas. Then, test them and see how well your predictions work. Don't just think your theory makes sense, test it. For example, is that really the reason I did what I did? Search for evidence based on your experiences beyond what you want or need to believe to be true.

Peer inside with an open mind, always searching for the truth. See if your notions and assumptions appear correct based on your experience – what happened, not what you think or would have liked to have happened.

Develop empathy

A great way to further enhance our understanding of feelings is to be curious about what others might feel and why. We aim to use our experiences as a frame of reference and ask what we must go through to act or behave like them. We can use a similar step-wise approach to understanding our feelings, observing, wondering and testing.

The test may be to sit down with the people whose feelings you are trying to understand and listen without judgement. We all have a tale to tell that can offer profound insights into feelings and why we feel and do what we do.

See what you can learn about the feelings of others by using your feelings and experiences as a reference – try to feel what they might be feeling and what led to them feeling this way. Try to understand their heart. Please don't be pushy; we must respect others' boundaries, but we can still be curious. Every understanding you gain about feelings, and every theory you validate about what we feel and why, will add to your wisdom.

It is okay if you don't feel confident yet using these four steps. In the next chapter, we will practice using them more when we delve into the mysterious feelings we know as love.

These simple steps for enhancing self-insight can also help us with big questions such as: what is my purpose? Why doesn't life make sense? It may take longer, but as long you are prepared to keep asking and developing your ideas and understandings about feelings, you will eventually find answers to why we act as we do. Remember, the old guy in the library does want to help us; he will show us what we want to see so long as we can convince him we want to know by persisting.

Try it. Ask questions about feelings as they relate to others so you can begin to understand their actions better. Try to feel what they may be going through to make them act as they do. Soon, you will understand their feelings and your own better.

Seeing a bigger picture and warnings

Make trying to understand feelings a project.

What feelings should I try to understand? Where should I look or start?

Begin with the feelings you are most curious about or want to change within yourself. Then, start with the feelings that you are experiencing now or today. The fresher the feeling, the easier it is to explore within it.

One of the beautiful side effects continuing to develop our understanding of feelings is that after a while, we may begin to see a broader picture of how feelings shape people, societies and events. We can start to feel how a more extensive picture can play a significant role in our feelings throughout our life and here and now, too – like how the behaviours of a government can affect how we feel and act. From being able to predict how one person feels and reacts, we begin to see how we might feel and respond as a larger group. I have found these broader insights can be alarming yet also empowering.

If there are warnings along the way, I will begin with these two. Firstly, be wary of making your explanations too broad. Secondly, avoid being dogmatic – being sure you are right.

Broad theories – such as 'It's all God's design' or 'It's just our flow of energy' – lack predictability and usefulness. Also, if we are sure we are right and feel compelled to convince others of our righteousness, then we can guarantee we are on the wrong track and are misguided. Truth, as we now know, is a process of personal refinement. It isn't an end goal or sudden realisation. Even my experience of The All I know was incomplete. (More on my connection with The All coming up soon ...)

In the search for understanding feelings, there is no room for vague ideas that offer us no useful predictions we can test. But, on the other hand, there is also no room for dogma to the point we need to tell everyone else we are the only person who knows what is right.

A final warning is don't give up any therapy and treatments for mental illnesses just because you have begun to understand feelings for yourself. Sure, you should feel comfortable with any treatments offered, but if your gut says this is wrong, listen to your gut – if you have the option. But no matter what therapies provide, you can still learn about feelings in the background. Therefore, I consider it safer to continue to consider the advice of the health professionals caring for you.

You might be wondering if, as you develop these insights and ideas, should you write them down as you go?

If you can develop your ideas and theories by writing them down as you go, feel free. I prefer to remember them as it keeps them in my mind to be processed even when I'm not focusing on them. Later, I will re-examine them and see if it is easier to understand or answer my query – I may have learned something new and relevant. I try to stick with one theory or idea at a time and try to answer it before moving on to the next, even if it takes weeks or more to sort. I wouldn't say

I like having too many balls in the air. Once I've made a discovery, I might spend weeks or more exploring it, how it has affected my life, how it may have impacted others, and how it might improve my life moving forward – no point in just dismissing something so valuable without squeezing something out of it.

Observe, question, theorise and test. Develop your ideas about how feelings work. Feelings have much they can teach us.

As mentioned earlier, in the following chapter, we will learn to apply some of the skills we have gained to understand love better. I should warn you that if the mystery of love makes it so appealing, I recommend you don't read the next chapter. On the other hand, suppose you want to understand love in a way that can enhance your life experience. In that case, I invite you to consider what you feel and experience of love.

We will also better understand how to communicate with feelings – by learning their language. This skill will put us much closer to being able to connect with The All directly.

CHAPTER 11

LOVE'S SECRETS LAID BARE

The metal edge of the curved-edged utensil pushes slowly against the hard cream-coloured ice, digging in deeper until a morsel is finally released and makes its way for a taste. Then, without a bite, it melts with smooth delight. I love ice-cream; rich chocolate is delightful. My current favourite is a mix of frozen strawberries with creamy vanilla. The fruit and dairy mix is so tempting I need to be careful how much I eat, or my waist proliferates. I love a soothing warm bath on a cold day. I love the fresh smell after the new rain. I love it when I can help someone be well, especially after many others have failed to help. I hold a gentle and subtle love for all that is. I have experienced the edges of romantic love and felt its incredible potential. The word 'love' can mean many things and represent even more feelings.

Lifting the veil of mysteries from love can be daunting, considering how quickly we use the word. Therefore, to simplify our job, we will work to understand better some of the feelings involved in romantic love, which sonnets are often written about.

We will use the steps and some skills we learned from the last chapter as our guide.

What has your experience of the feelings of love so far been? Perhaps you experienced deep attraction for someone you only just met? Or a deep affection and warmth for the one holding you in their arms? Maybe, ecstasy at the realisation this could be the partner you would be overjoyed to be with for the rest of your life? We may feel it in fantasy and powerful desire. Some of us may know these feelings well; others might only know them through dreams, stories and movies. Others still may need to learn what feelings we are talking about. But, no matter our experience of the feelings of romantic love – or lack thereof – we can still gain great wisdom from them by asking the golden question.

Love and the golden question

What do your feelings of romantic love want from you? Do you know? For instance, you are head over heels for someone you just met; your palms sweat and your heart pounds. What do these feelings within the wonderful attraction want you to do precisely? How can we find out?

By now, you would have realised that every feeling is composed of other feelings. So what might some of these feelings be that speak to us so loudly, with powerful new attraction? Let us begin by breaking down the feelings into two types, as we have done previously – the feelings of fear and desire. By understanding these feelings, we can also better understand what a stable, satisfying relationship looks like and how to achieve it.

Fear's embrace

How much of the powerful experience of chemistry with that person you are magnetically attracted to is recognisable as fear? Look inside your heart; what do you notice? Do you feel afraid? The sweaty palms and racing heart are a giveaway – part of the fear response. So yes, often, this kind of powerful initial feeling of love – attraction – can be terrifying. But what might we be afraid of? What scenarios scare you about them the most?

You will recall we learned earlier that we feel fear because our brain is considering future scenarios. What scenarios are triggering anxiety here? For instance, are you terrified you won't be able to resist them? Are you scared they won't like you and fear the pain of rejection? Are you fearful you might embarrass yourself, and the best life opportunity for lasting love will disappear? Could it be all of the above or some others?

Only you can know what scares you about your deep attraction to someone. Once you recognise the fear, it is up to you to decide whether you want to be so afraid. If not, then working to resolve your worries is the next sensible step using some of the skills we previously mentioned – what is your plan? Can you accept the worst case?

If you want to avoid looking at the fear and seek to revel in the intensity of its potential terror, then it is best to avoid looking at the fear and instead embrace it. But, on the other hand, if the fear is so bad it prevents you from taking the next step, you might want to work to reduce your anxiety by at least a little.

It is worth reminding ourselves that powerful chemistry or strong attraction does not mean we will find romantic bliss together. Fear can add a new intensity to the attraction, but that doesn't mean our romance will last or be deeply satisfying – more about that in a moment.

If there isn't much fear involved in your initial meetings, that is fine too; a satisfying, stable love doesn't have to terrify us or begin with terror at the start. Some long-term, satisfying relationships begin with loathing.

What other feelings are involved early in our relationship and as it progresses? Let us look at the feelings associated with desires and what role they might play.

Love desires – yes, please

Romantic love is filled to the brim with desire; that's the point. And it has the reward of ecstasy and pleasure as we've never imagined. The flip side to the immense joy, unfortunately, is excruciating agony. What we feel is likely to be somewhere in between. Suppose we want more of the ecstasy and pleasure and less of the suffering. In that case, we will want to know what this myriad of desires wants from us so we can fully realise its potential.

Do you know what your love desires want from you?

How do we make sense of so many love-related desires and feelings? We can use the BOS Model, once again, as our guide.

Which of the three human essences in the BOS Model can we expect to encompass most of our desires and feelings of romantic love? That would be Family Self. After all, we are not trying to have a relationship with ourselves – Personal Self related desires – and we aren't having a romantic relationship with a whole community; we, for the most part, are trying to have a romantic relationship with one person above all else. Family Self desires, you may recall, are specific desires to drive us to be part of a family and have our own family. Romantic love forms part of the foundational desires that help us build a stable, satisfying family.

So, when we meet that special person for the first time, what can we expect our Family Self desires to want us to do? For starters, to get close to them and be noticed by them, so we can meet, talk and see each other again. The more attraction we have for them, the harder it will be to get them out of our minds.

It can be maddening; we can be at work, with family, talking to friends and one person keeps popping up in our mind. If we have the courage, we might take the next step or wait for them to make the next move. If they don't call or act, we can feel terrible; what did I do wrong? Don't they like me enough? They could be thinking the same about us.

Initiating relationships these days seems so complicated, yet what our feelings want from us is very basic – to meet up and get to know each other, and see if we can get along.

What feelings have you noticed early in your past relationships or the ones you aspired to that never worked out? What did they want from you? What did they want you to do?

Was there sexual attraction from the start? What images went through your mind that aroused you to the point of needing to act? Or were you too scared or cautious? As you are beginning to realise, feelings are associated with scenarios. So when attracted to someone, what scenarios is your mind playing out – what dreams and fantasies? How do these scenarios make you feel? What do they want you to do?

But are there only sexual feelings in romantic love? Some might say so, but experience and internal searching tell us other feelings are also at play.

Let me ask you a question to help clarify some of the other desires and feelings at work. How important is a deep, close friendship to a long, stable and satisfying relationship? Search your feelings – what do they say? Almost everyone I've asked this question to – bar one – said friendship was essential. Okay, are we really in romantic love with someone if they can't be our close friend? Probably not.

In other words, romantic love is not just about sexual attraction; an enduring, satisfying love that gives us the greatest pleasure and contentment is with a close friend. That means many of the feelings love wants us to satisfy are our friendship desires – desires of Community Self. In other words, if we don't feel respected, cared for, appreciated, supported, heard, valued, protected and noticed, and have a sense of commonality as well as feeling validated, we will not feel the deepest, most satisfied feelings of romantic love we are capable of.

How well are your friendship needs being met in your relationship? For example, do you feel close, cared for, heard, respected and appreciated? When was your last intimate date and close, meaningful open chat? How well were these friendship needs met in past relationships – could you be close friends and have fun together?

The need for friendship desires to be fulfilled in romantic love also highlights the point that just because we are sexually attracted to another person doesn't mean we can be close friends. We can't be close friends with everyone; some of us, through no fault of either party, won't be able to get along.

It is in recognising how critical friendship desires are in fulfilling romantic love that I consider we aren't in love until we get to know each other and still feel mutual love – usually after many months and preferably at least a year. Until then, our feelings are lust, not yet true romantic love.

Are there any other desires at play in romantic love? There most definitely are.

For instance, Community Self desires from outside the relationship can play a decisive role. The traits our society says are attractive will impact who and what we are attracted to. For example, if society likes thin people, we are more likely to be attracted to thin people. Suppose our community is attracted to wealth and power. In that case, we are more likely to be attracted to wealth, power, and the trends the rich and powerful set – such as celebrity fashions and appearances. Community Self desires remind us those around us heavily influence us. We can expect traits we find attractive, appealing or endearing in our partner to be affected – consciously or unconsciously – by our peers or those we aspire to be like.

We can also feel unsatisfied with our partner if they don't fit in or impress our friends, or social and family group. Search inside your feelings. Are there any feelings in your relationship that drive you to want to fit in?

How can we be sure our partner loves us for who we are and not what we bring to the table? Ultimately, we can't until we lose everything, and they are still there. But we can get an idea of the influence of others by asking if we would still feel satisfied with our partner if no one ever knew we were together. How do you feel about your partner if the views of others didn't play any role in your feelings for them?

As you can see, romantic love has many desires from within many aspects of our lives. If you wish to explore them in more detail, I outline them in greater depth in the book *The Fall and Rise of Women, How Women Can Change the World*. By better understanding the desires involved in romantic relationships, we better understand the feelings associated with them and how to find fulfilment.

What about the desires of Personal Self? Do they play a role in romantic love?

Absolutely.

Personal Self desires play such a critical role we will consider them soon. But first, we will learn more about feelings in relationships by shining a flashlight of truth into the dark.

Love's dark truths

It would be magnificent if all love were bright, uplifting, warm and nourishing to our very being. But, unfortunately, there can also be dark, traumatic, miserable and soul-destroying love. Because we may have unrealistic romantic notions of love, we can use the idea or word 'love' as an excuse for the inexcusable. We may think we love or are in love when it isn't what most consider functional and satisfying love. Consider the following examples of dark love and some of the feelings involved.

Examples of dark love

How many of the following examples resonate or currently apply for you? Perhaps, like me, you have experienced more than one type?

Controlling love

Honey, I'm only making you do it because I love you and want the best. Can't you see that? Just do what I say, and you'll be fine.

The key to any form of positive and functional love is respect. Respect is founded on equality – treating each other as equals. At the core of respect is choice. If we have no choice, such as being coerced, emotionally blackmailed or threatened with punishment, our partner is not respecting us. We will consider the vital link between respect and choice when we considering strong foundations for self in a moment.

Similarly, we do not genuinely respect our partners if we put them on a pedestal or if they do the same for us. Adoring or completely idolising someone to the point of them no longer being equal is not meeting each other's needs for respect.

Unfortunately, it is easy to find ourselves in controlling relationships within modern society. If our society is hierarchical, our families and relationships are more likely to be hierarchical. One person takes charge and gives orders. We are also tempted to take control when we are short on time, under the pump, and things have to get done – fear drives us. I don't have time to discuss it; do what I say!

But when we remove a person's sense of choice, we also lessen their sense of Personal Self. As we lose our sense of self, we often become less attractive in our partner's eyes. The less attractive we become, the less satisfied our partner can be with us and the less fulfilling our relationship. Becoming less attractive in our partner's eyes can easily trigger frustration, anger and disinterest.

But I still love them. Suppose you have come to an arrangement where one person dominates or controls the relationship, and you can both accept it. In that case, that is a personal choice. It can make sense to be with a dominating figure; they can help us feel safe, and we don't have to take on the burden of making decisions and getting them wrong. But beware – the other person's control could mean we quickly lose ourselves. Once that happens, we can begin to emotionally detach and struggle to find satisfaction in many different aspects of life. So control and domination in relationships come with a sting in the tail we must be wary of.

Do you feel your partner is controlling you? Do you feel you need to be submissive to keep the peace? How is this controlling behaviour affecting you or your partner's sense of self and self-esteem? How is being controlled influencing your feelings within the relationship, and what the feelings want you to do?

Co-dependent love

Positive love should help us grow and take on the world confidently, not restrict and hold us back. However, a co-dependent love is restrictive and suppressive by its nature.

What do we mean by co-dependence?

In a classic co-dependent relationship, there is a victim and a saviour. The victim needs to stay disempowered and helpless, so the saviour will show care and affection by saving them. The saviour needs the victim to remain disempowered. Hence, they feel the other person needs them and appreciates what they give. The saviour gets satisfaction from helping the victim. The victim gets pleasure from being saved. Both of them hold back the victim from being independent and growing as a human being and contribute to the victim losing their sense of self.

In romantic relationships, wherever one person is disempowered, a dark love is taking place, not a positive love of light and growth.

Will we necessarily be aware we are in a co-dependent relationship? Often, we may not. We can be used to the dynamic or not recognise it from the start.

A GP at a CBT training conference I once attended shared important advice about love her father once gave her. Don't mistake feeling sorry for someone as love, he told her. It is golden advice. Feeling sorry for our partner and interpreting sorrow as love can easily lead to co-dependence.

Do you feel sorry for your partner? Do you feel the need to save them? Are you scared your partner will leave you if you become strong and independent? Is this how you want romantic love to be and feel for you?

Abusive love

I cannot tell you how many times a person has come to see me and told me they are being abused – either physically, verbally, emotionally, or all three – and yet they then say, 'But I love them'. It is more common with an alcoholic partner; the partner has a bender, and then out comes Mr Hyde – Dr Jekyll's nasty alter ego. I love them when they aren't drunk; they're a good person. I love them when they aren't in a rage. But during the rage and intoxication, toxic abuse reigns.

The truth is these people's abusive partners choose the abuse. They decide to drink, knowing they will be abusive. They choose not to control their rage or seek help for it. And each time the victim of the abuse shows love for them afterwards, and the abusive behaviour is validated and continues.

Abuse can take many forms, from gaslighting to putting you down to saying 'What would you know?' It could be dismissing your concerns without listening. It is abuse when we give the silent treatment and do not talk to someone for weeks or months. Suppose someone's finances are controlled so they can't access them without permission. That's abusive control. Neglect is also a powerful form of abuse: intentionally withholding emotional support and not meeting emotional needs. Abuse can take many forms; it doesn't have to be physical.

Are you feeling abused in your relationship? Are you the one doing the abuse?

The bottom line is if there is abuse in the relationship, it is not a positive, loving relationship; it is dark love, damaging and ultimately soul-destroying. It doesn't matter how often they say they love you; the truth is in action. The good news is help is available – for example, men's support groups and counselling. Call the appropriate authorities if you feel in immediate danger – we deserve to feel safe.

Sometimes people outside of dark-love relationships wonder why the victims stay. There can be many reasons, chief among them can be fear.

As we have seen, we are made to be afraid of the unknown. We can stay within abusive relationships because they are familiar. We can remain because of threats made against us if we leave. We can hold onto the dark love because it may be the only love we know, and we are resigned to it. For instance, we may have grown up with abuse and are drawn to it because we believe it is what we deserve. We may have suffered abuse so long that we believe our abuser when they say no one else would ever want to love us. There are innumerable reasons we stay or even seek out dark love.

And as we immerse ourselves within dark love's grip, we can easily find we try to keep busy to avoid the feelings we don't want to confront; we can avoid looking at our difficulties or deny these negative feelings exist; we can take up an addiction; and we can detach emotionally to try to cope. We are trying not to shine a light of truth into the shadows.

How many feelings of love within you are negative feelings lurking in the shadows waiting for resolution? How many seek help so we can finally cast them aside and have the positive and uplifting love we deserve?

Truly understanding romantic love is shining the light of truth into our darkest feelings so we can grow from transforming them.

Strong foundations of self

Do you ever feel that you need more time to yourself in your relationship? Time to gather your thoughts, consider the feelings in your heart and get some space away from the influence of others. Perhaps you feel guilty for making this time, or someone shows their disapproval. But how can we hope to build and maintain a joyous romantic love if we don't build it on deep and stable foundations?

Personal Self related feelings can be considered our compass to a more profound honesty that allows the most fulfilling love to blossom and thrive.

To help us better understand the importance and role of feelings related to Personal Self, let us consider in more detail what Personal Self represents and how it can directly impact our satisfaction.

Personal Self, as described in the BOS Model, is broken down into five parts: self-worth, self-respect, having a sense of choice, being your own best friend, and knowing what you think and feel in your own right. How do these apply to the feelings and satisfaction we experience in a relationship?

Enduring self-worth

Self-worth is where our needs come in the scheme of things; are we putting our needs first, second or last? I often find parents, for instance, put their needs last and fair enough. In a family, the first person's needs we usually sacrifice are our own, the next our partner's, and the last is our children's. Nature created this impulse on purpose, so our children would survive. But nature also gave us this feeling assuming we would have the support of a tribe. In a supportive tribe, the rest of the tribe would actively ensure our needs are met too. That is no longer the case; society expects us to raise our families and meet our needs independently. But sacrifice our needs too much, and we can forget what we like anymore. We also make ourselves unattractive to our partners.

Have you ever been out socially and scanned the room? Who were the most attractive people? The ones who always follow what others do and have no individual or original thoughts or ideas, or those with a strong sense of self, who know their likes, dislikes and views, and respect themselves? A robust Personal Self gives off an energy of confidence others can notice. Who wants to spend their life with someone who keeps asking you what they should like and always agrees with you? It can drive you nuts.

Sacrifice too much of ourselves in a relationship by not seeking to meet our own needs, and we lose our attractive appeal. We also become someone different from the person our partner was attracted to and fell in love with. Our self-worth must endure for each of us in the relationship to feel satisfied.

Does that mean our needs should come first in a relationship? No – a solid Personal Self, with an honest connection to our own desires, seeks a balance. Create and maintain this balance, and our partner will also be more satisfied with us, and we are more likely to be happy with them if they do the same.

What are your feelings of self-worth wanting you to do?

Ever-deserved self-respect and sense of choice

Self-worth ensures we prioritise our human needs and desires in life. Self-respect, by contrast, primarily asks us to focus on looking after our physical and psychological integrity and well-being. A critical component of self-respect is having a strong sense of choice.

Why is a sense of choice so fundamental to self-respect, and how do these two components affect feelings in our romantic relationships?

Let us briefly clarify the fundamental link between respect and a sense of choice.

Consider the example of an enslaved person and enslaver. When an enslaver tells the enslaved person to do something, does the enslaved person have a choice? Not really; if they don't do what the enslaver demands, the enslaver will severely punish them – saying no isn't an option. Is the enslaved person being respected by the enslaver by being given no choice? No. Having a sense of choice – being able to say no without any punishment – is critical to being respected.

In other words, respect is predicated on a sense of equality – no one is superior to us in any way, certainly not to the point they are allowed to dominate us and make us disregard our feelings and desires.

We all need and deserve respect – it can be considered a human right – since without it we cannot realise the full potential of our existence as a human being. How can we come to enjoy the satisfactions of life if we aren't even allowed to consider fulfilling them? If only those superior to us can satisfy their desires, how does that help us realise ours? It ultimately doesn't.

When we take away our ability to choose, we rob ourselves of the emotional connection required for deeply satisfying relationships.

Do you feel you are in a relationship with an equal? Do you ask your partner to do something and then indicate disappointment? Roll your eyes and punish them for saying no? Do you always have a plan B so you know it is okay for your partner to say no to your requests? Does your partner allow you to refuse their requests without any punishment? How does not being given a real choice to say no feel?

Let us take the critical link between choice and respect and how it affects our feelings further.

If no one seems to respect us, why should we respect ourselves? More often than not, how others treat us affects how we treat ourselves. If they treat us well, we are more likely to treat ourselves well. But let our self-respect fall, and we can expect to no longer care for our physical and mental well-being as we know we should. Why even shower or care for personal hygiene and fitness – no one seems to care anyway. Then how lousy do we feel?

But in relationships, respect works both ways. If we respect ourselves, we can help our partners feel respected. The opinions of people who show no respect for themselves mean less to us. Next thing, our partner loses attraction to us because they don't feel respected enough by us, simply because we don't indicate *we* respect us.

By losing respect for ourselves and each other, we open ourselves to dark love, such as co-dependence and abuse, as mentioned previously. Soon, we can fall into a victim role. And when our partner abuses us, we will likely suffer the abuse again because we don't respect ourselves enough to defend and protect ourselves.

Self-respect is satisfying feelings for self-care, health and wellbeing and meeting our needs. It is about ensuring we maintain a sense of choice as a priority. Respect ourselves, and we respect our humanity and humanity everywhere. At the same time, we help our partners to be respected and maintain the attraction of a close friendship.

Maintaining a strong sense of self-worth and self-respect are also measures of being our own best friend. If we can't treat ourselves with the love of a good friend, how can we expect anyone else to, let alone our partner?

> **How strong are your feelings of self-respect? Do you feel like you have a sense of choice in your life and relationship? Can you notice feelings within that seek for you to care for yourself better? What are these feelings asking you to do?**

Knowing your thoughts and feelings

Increasing our sense of Personal Self in a romantic sense begins by breaking free of our community's dysfunctional views, expectations and ideals and rediscovering the truth of the feelings of our heart, including those of greater love and erotic arousal. It means exploring and listening deeply to what nature wants of us – physically, emotionally and spiritually. It also means accepting the responsibility of self-control.

One of the critical insights I gained through connection with The All was the realisation we are far more than purely physical beings; the physical is but a small fraction of our greater non-physical – often called spiritual – sense. As a reflection of our non-physical being, we can tap into a profound and infinitely expansive love for all things, either intensely emotional or ephemeral and subtle, existing within our deeper being. This expansive love is a will of greater joy, well-being and completeness for all beings and existence. This spiritual type of love – for want of another way to describe it – can form the foundation of all romantic love and is worth embracing and embellishing. To know the feelings of romantic love is to understand the feelings of a non-critical love, always accepting and centred in permanent goodwill, no matter our disagreements.

How can we know and enhance our spiritual type of love?

A straightforward way to enhance these feelings is through meditation. For example, sit quietly and visualise you have a warm heart of immense goodwill for all beings. Next, imagine enveloping all beings, every creature, plant and area of the country, within its warm embrace. Try to be specific about the creatures and places – give detail, and make it as accurate as possible. Next, offer this same love for your partner or prospective partner and notice how it feels. How does it change your reaction and feelings about them? How do these feelings impact your closeness?

Living in a competitive and often brutal world, we can quickly lose sight and connection with our sense of greater love and goodwill. Unless we practise connecting with it, we may forget it is there.

Of course, we are also physical beings with cravings and potential feelings of great pleasure. Nature has physical wants for us in our romantic love. How do we know what nature wants us to do in romantic love? We can peer into our feelings and find out.

For instance, in the privacy of our homes, we can explore erotic and primal feelings. We can intimately know these desires and what they seek of us using our imagination and fantasies – for example, imagining our primal erotic urges being allowed to arise without constraint, having complete control and rising without limit. What feelings and images then arise? What is nature wanting us to do?

Raising Personal Self and knowing our true selves is breaking free of society's influence and prudishness and knowing our heart – including the most primal, arousing feelings and images and embracing them. It is like learning to master fear; it is the powerful fears we don't allow ourselves to realise and master that control and dominate us. Similarly, it is the feelings and urges of an erotic nature and arousal we aren't prepared to acknowledge and embrace that trigger us and can dominate our lives. Knowing and accepting our most primal erotic urges and drives allows us room to embrace a part of ourselves society doesn't want to be expressed; but, simultaneously, learning enough of the feelings means to take greater control of them. We will discuss more about the value of control relating to certain romantic feelings in a moment.

Don't judge these feelings and imaginings; notice and explore them. Should we be willing, we can create other imaginative scenarios and explore further. For example, imagine there are erotic energies we can all tap into, far more potent than physical sex. Powers that can be set free in each of us, like tapping into a mighty and endless river of erotic arousal. Use whatever imaginings and fantasies you wish. Once the feelings are in your presence, it is up to you to embrace and explore them, seek to understand them, or both. Creating scenarios helps us know what nature wants of us and its intent.

Aside from imaginings, we have physical bodies, too. To raise our Personal Self within feelings of romantic love is also to explore and embrace the sensual. This exploration, in turn, can increase our connection with our feminine and masculine selves and allow us to know them intimately.

For example, as a woman, what is it like to feel your sensual being and set it free to be fully realised and expressed? What deep pleasures is nature asking you to discover, so you feel true to yourself?

Similarly, as a man, what sensual and erotic feelings is nature seeking you to embrace? Is it found with greater strength and a sense of dominance? Are there erotic feelings that give deep pleasure with less physical touch and gentle kindness?

Other than better understanding these feelings, there is another powerful reason to explore these erotic and sensual experiences. It can be hard to share with our partner what we don't recognise in ourselves. In other words, the more we know what satisfies us, the more we can share and explore with our partner. The greater the deep pleasures of romantic feelings we share and explore as a couple, the more potential for interpersonal growth and maintenance of a lasting bond.

Exploring the erotic and romantic to enhance our relationships is not new. For instance, we find examples in the Kama Sutra and Tantric sex. In addition, the Greeks opened themselves to exploring these feelings by creating the myth of Psyche and Eros and worshipping Aphrodite, the goddess of love and fertility.

To know the truth of what we feel in our own right is to acknowledge and embrace the sensual and erotic feelings in their purity within ourselves. However, to let these feelings arise without learning control would be profoundly unwise, hence the need to know personal control.

Let all our erotic feelings and imaginings go wild in a society of dominance and punishment, and we are asking for chaos and enormous suffering. To know our Personal Self romantic feelings is to take responsibility for them in the bigger picture – within a framework of balance and long-term harmony. How can we take control of such powerful feelings without suppressing them to the point of them becoming an obsession and controlling us? We have several options.

Firstly, we recognise the critical importance of respect. We respect ourselves, so we do no permanent harm to ourselves, and especially, we respect others. So, for instance, it is not okay to support sexual slavery, paedophilia and sexual exploitation online or otherwise.

Responsible control of our romantic feelings means respect for our relationships. As we noted, nature wants us to develop a strong bond with a partner to build a stable family to meet our children's needs better and ensure their survival. We disrespect relationships through infidelity and risk the foundations of family stability. We also threaten our health and social cohesion.

Just because we have powerful erotic feelings doesn't permit us to act on them without consideration for others and our health – we can still get STIs. And promiscuity can lead to jealousy and anger, resentment and betrayal. Not to mention tearing our families apart.

Responsible control of our romantic feelings can also mean being careful about who we fantasise about. For instance, if they are someone we know socially or at work and are unavailable or uninterested, it may make our days awkward. In addition, because we hold the images in our mind, the temptation becomes to act out the fantasy and threaten their or our current family or relationship integrity. In that case, we may wish to redirect our erotic imaginings and explorations elsewhere. Or learn how to switch them off.

How do we switch off romantic or erotic feelings?

We create scenarios that are unpleasant and have unsavoury outcomes. In other words, we recognise the link between feelings and scenarios, and use images of the other person that are repulsive in some way or imagine consequences we know we don't want and let ourselves feel them. For instance, if we know such enacted fantasies would see us lose our valued job, career or family, we picture the consequences happening and allow ourselves to feel the outcome. That way, we create a negative feeling associated with the fantasy, which no longer becomes a scenario worth indulging in.

Our responsibility is to control our feelings about someone and how we react. Many scenario-creating techniques make that possible, including remembering we are in control of our behaviours. No one, and no being – supernatural or otherwise – ultimately controls our actions. Being around someone may trigger certain feelings within us, but it is then up to us how we respond to them – it's our responsibility.

So, we should explore our erotic, sensual and spiritual feelings or romantic love in the privacy of our homes and get to know them well. Then we must remind ourselves of the bigger picture – romantic feelings aren't just about us. Raising Personal Self using feelings of romantic love is recognising we have other desires seeking to be balanced within us in a harmonious way too.

What are your romantic, erotic, sensual and spiritual feelings wanting from you? What is nature asking you to do through your feelings, and why?

Relatable love empathy and enquiry

We take romantic love to a whole new level when we try to make sense of the feelings of our partners, the opposite sex, and by making understanding love our pet project.

Let's admit it – sometimes our partners or the opposite sex don't make sense. So what's wrong with them? Nothing. We just haven't created scenarios with feelings in them – understandings – that make them predictable yet.

How can we make our partners and the opposite sex more understandable and predictable?

We can begin by talking to them and trying to understand their perspective. Try to understand what scenarios made them feel as they do both in their past and now. We do this without judgement, simply trying to connect the dots. We also do it knowing we are all allowed to learn from our mistakes; the person we were does not necessarily mean we are the same person today. So we tread softly, with a caring heart.

In addition, we can let our hearts drift into their feelings and what we sense in them. As we understand and explore feelings more, we can sense the stories behind their feelings, almost as if we have a sixth sense. We can always check if we are close by asking.

Suppose we still don't know what is going on in their heart and why they act as they do; what next?

Suppose you are a man trying to understand better the romantic and other feelings in a woman's heart. In that case, consider and discuss them as you read about them in books such as *The Fall and Rise of Women*. Learn what women's priorities are, how they have been treated, and the prejudices and injustices against them – often by men – and you will soon begin to get the picture, if you are open to learning.

Similarly, suppose men don't make sense. In that case, we can try to explore their primary driving desires in a world driven by wealth, status and power. They were brought up to believe a man has to lead as well as support the family; they've never been taught to discuss or understand what is in their hearts; and they're confused about how they are supposed to behave, especially around women. The modern world is challenging for men, too. We all struggle to find a deep satisfaction with each other that works for us.

By making our partner or the opposite sex more understandable by better getting to know their heart, it also makes us closer. The more we discern what our partner feels, the stronger our bond of care and trust can become.

'But my man still doesn't know about feelings – now what?' I hear some of you say.

We don't put pressure on them to express their feelings. Instead, we explore scenarios with them, what they notice from these scenarios, and what those feelings make them want to do. We focus on the actions behind the feelings, not the words.

In other words, we increase their feeling literacy.

Those of us who have kept away from feelings are often scared we will be humiliated or our feelings will be used against us, so any discussion of feelings must come with no hint of sarcasm or ridicule. Instead, feelings must be validated: 'Yes, I'd probably have felt and reacted the same.' We link how others treated them to what feelings arose and how they felt like acting – we help them connect the dots. The more scenarios we relate to feelings, the more we improve the other person's EQ (emotional quotient), and yet at no time do we have to struggle to put names to what we feel or name the emotion.

How well do you know the feelings and scenarios behind and currently in your partner's life?

Suppose we want to take our understanding of feelings to another level still – to the point where we can develop deep wisdom that we can pass on. Why not make understanding romantic feelings a new project?

Let us call it My Love Project.

My Love Project

When you discover something new about the feelings of love, either make a mental note or write it down. This exploration is our search for the truth of what we and others feel in love and how it impacts our behaviours and actions. As we refine our views and develop our understanding, we can create a bigger picture that makes sense, linking the ideas or theories to what nature wants of us from romantic love and why. The bigger picture becomes increasingly complete as we search for our sense of truth about love – what feels profoundly true for us.

Most of my understanding of the feelings of love has come from a similar approach to the one just mentioned. I also learned from discussions with specialist counsellors about their practices. I sought to understand them based on my frameworks to see if they correlated or could work. We have many sources open to us to understand the feelings of love better.

The bottom line, though, is we still need to base our understanding on our experiences first and foremost. We adapt our ideas rather than discard them for others. We continue to search for what feels true and never let ourselves get caught in the traps we mentioned earlier, of being dogmatic and imposing our ideas on others.

Be curious about a romantic or erotic feeling you notice. Explore inside it. Ask it questions and create theories as to why this might be so. Then test the theory by looking at your past and current experiences or what others share with you. Does your idea make others more predictable and understandable? If it does, then it suggests you are on the right track. Persist, and your wisdom founded on understanding feelings will increase.

Try not to be discouraged and be put off by shadows from the past. Often, it is resolving our shadows that can help our relationships the most. For example, if we were abandoned as a child or ignored – emotional abuse – this can continue to impact us today and make us needy and clingy. We may have suffered one or more partners' infidelity and find it hard to trust or commit to someone wonderful. Our tragic past may have us convinced we are unlovable. So we sabotage our relationships just as they look like they will be amazing.

As I learned long ago, the story we believe about us is the one we try to validate. Suppose we have a negative view of ourselves. In that case, it can profoundly impact the depth and satisfaction of any relationship. Sometimes, we must rewrite who we are by rewriting our past traumas and pivotal events. If we can't do this ourselves, we shouldn't hesitate to seek professional help.

By now, some of you may have realised we have already been learning the language of feelings. What this language is and how it can help connect us to The All we will consider next. We will also clarify some of the nature of The All experience – what is it?

When I had that transcendent experience in my mid-twenties, had I connected with God? Could feelings genuinely offer us a way to transform our lives and take the development of the world into a finer, more advanced age? To answer these critical questions, first, I would read some books that held a new interest. Unusual for me; I only read a few books a year and only non-fiction.

CHAPTER 12

COULD THE ALL BE GOD?

Let me be frank – after my experience of connection with The All, I became an atheist. I had grown up Catholic, been through the rituals of receiving my first holy communion, went through the process of confirmation, and had read the bible several times – though not to the point of memorising it. What others taught me about God was so at odds with the nature of the experience of The All, I dismissed notions of a Christian or any other religion's version of God out of hand. Then, gradually, I began to read books that held a new interest for me, and one especially made me question my assumptions. What if I was wrong and The All and God were the same? More than that, what if all the great beliefs and religions of the past were all representations of trying to interpret the same thing – the same source? But how could that be?

The book that made me return to reconsider my transcendent experience the most was *Sacred Nature: How we can recover our bond with the natural world*. The author, Karen Armstrong, is a highly regarded expert and commentator on religious affairs. She was a Catholic nun for six years until, in 1969, she left her teaching order to read English at St Anne's College, Oxford. As I read the book, I could see she had been on a personal quest that saw her intimately know the concepts and intricacies of many of the world's philosophies and religions – her expertise in the subject was extensive and personal.

Sacred Nature aims to restore our emotional connection to nature. If we connect emotionally to it, then we are more likely to care for and respect it. Armstrong recognised, quite rightly, we live in a world dominated by the emotional detachment of logic – the left brain – as opposed to the bigger picture-focused and more emotionally engaged right brain: too much logos, not enough mythos. So we went from listening to those who felt an emotional connection with nature and developed a wholistic relationship with it filled with mythology to breaking nature down into unemotive smaller bits with forces we could manipulate and control. So how did this book change my view of my experience with The All and God?

The book offered many summaries of how religions from Christianity to Islam, Hinduism, Daoism, Buddhism and more all had shown evidence of a deep emotional connection with the natural world. What struck me most was the descriptions of some of the founders' experiences I didn't know before, and how our Western view of God had gone from God being within all nature, hence nature being divine and to be respected, to God becoming a distant figure ruling from some other remote place. What I read resonated in ways I wasn't expecting. The first revelations came from a summary of the origins of Daoism.

I had already developed an interest in Chinese history and thought by this point. As previously mentioned, the Chinese, over thousands of years, had tried many systems – including beliefs – to contain the damaging influences of our greed – that is, our desire for wealth, power and status. However, I hadn't studied the exact origins of some of these beliefs, other than a cursory look at Confucianism, Daoism generally, and many myths inherent in the tales of Buddha. Now I was learning about Laozi, the 4th-century BCE founder of Daoism.

Laozi, I learned, describes himself as an outsider regarded by the 'clever' people as clumsy, gloomy and uncouth. He hailed from a people who had maintained rich, colourful mythology and tribal shamanistic traditions; they had remained close to rivers, mountains, wild marshes and forests. Laozi revived ancient notions of Dao, a sacred principle of nature. He also experienced an enigmatic vision.

Through what Armstrong describes as a 'contemplative and intuitive state of mind,' Laozi glimpsed a 'dynamic, sacred force at the heart of mundane existence.' He would later describe his experience in the enigmatic verses of the *Daodejing*, which can be translated as 'The Classic of the Way and its Power'.

> The way (dao) that can be spoken of
> is not the constant way;
> The name that can be named
> is not the constant name.
> The nameless was the beginning of heaven and
> earth.
> The named was the mother of the myriad
> Creatures (wanwu).

Laozi implies that what he experienced cannot be explained with words, but he then describes some of its qualities. For instance, all things have their origin in this sacred source and will return to it. The Dao is described as a force that holds everything together, makes it work and makes it productive. There is no creator who controls things from afar; we are all of Dao. There is no implication that we are a creation of domination or power. Ultimately, we are all but transitory manifestations of the Dao in a different form – in our case, a human manifestation.

But the human form seems to be the only creature as a manifestation of the Dao that can distort the sacred identity. We do this with our egos. So how do we see past the distortion to how things really are? A contemporary Daoist philosopher, Zhuangzi (369–286 BCE), recommended we do it by observing the Dao in nature. Until we 'forget' ourselves, we don't experience transcendence.

Other beliefs also capture the ineffable nature of a force that animates us, that we are part of and return to. For instance, in the ancient texts of Hinduism, the Vedas describe through colourful poetry the Rta as an 'active, creative truth' and the 'the way things truly are.' The Rta became replaced in a new spiritual movement by the Brahmin, the only Atman ('self') of the universe that permeated everything and everyone, living in each and every being. Whether it is Dao, Rta, the Brahmin or *qi*, the energy that manifests all things through a balance of opposing forces of yin and yang, there seems to remain an image within us of an all-encompassing force or being we are part of, and return to – an experience that is difficult to truly realise.

Another person's experience of transcendence I found particularly useful to reconsider was that of Siddhartha Gautama, later recognised as the Buddha.

Even though I read and considered many Buddhist concepts and mythology over the years, it was in *Sacred Nature* that I read an interpretation I hadn't noticed before.

If I was to summarise, Buddha reached his transcendence in a series of steps of benevolence. In his final step, he had to abandon all personal interests and transcend himself in an act of love to all other beings. The vehicle to self-disconnect was limitless love and a projection of endless well-being and joy for everything. I assume the writings accurately represent his experience, not an idealised version or mythology.

Sages over the ages have recognised that transcendence requires a disconnect from the ego. Once achieved, they try to explain what they have achieved and how others might reach the same. In all described accounts, unless we lose ourselves, we don't see or experience the completeness that is the truth of all things.

Was there ever a time when we regarded God within all beings – that we were part of His greater being? Apparently, yes, as *Sacred Nature* enlightens us, as to how it used to be. And Jesus seemed to recognise the need to give up the ego in our spiritual quest noting that 'a grain of wheat must fall to the ground and die before it bore fruit.'

Reading every page of *Sacred Nature* was like being intentionally reminded of my experience of The All. Every description and path to trying to realise the truth resonated. Had I disregarded and found a way to disconnect from my ego? Yes, I had, but my steps differed from those I read.

How did I detach from myself to realise – not just imagine but feel part of and know – beyond and The All?

I needed to transcend emotional pain or hurt – let it go and understand it to the point it wasn't significant. I needed to transcend fear. If I had any fears, they would affect what I could notice.

The point of giving up ego came once I was prepared to face nonexistence – to begin to totally immerse myself in not being at all. In that one acceptance, I disconnected from all fear and desire. I allowed myself to be nothing, extremely close to the point of likely actual death. But in a way, I had died; all that was and could have been did die.

We have begun to see our feelings manifest as fears and desires that guide our experiences as human beings. They also restrict what we can see – we can only see within the limits of what we are afraid of and what will cause us joy or pain. Our potential experience of everything is narrowed down by our human feelings of fear and desire, as if focused like a beam of light through a lens – a vastly broader light becoming narrow and intense – from the greater everything. Our feelings narrow the experience, but they do so for practical reasons.

Our place in nature guides our fears and emotional pains. Nature needs us to do certain things to be part of its harmonious balance – eat, drink, reproduce, etc. Our feelings and the choices that link to them reflect our humanity and the choice of experiencing this physical being – the choice of being human. Without desires and fears, we would die. But fears and desires aren't all we are. As all these sages have reminded us, we can perceive much more and know a greater truth once we disconnect from the desires inherent in creating our human form or ego.

How is it we can know such truth?

My best description – it may change over time – is that once we remove the restrictions that focus us as humans, we can perceive our greater being or a representation of it. For example, we can live and love the people around us, and all we have accumulated and achieved seems to be very successful according to society's standards. We can even revel in this experience. But once we see past the fears and desires that have defined our life, past what we think is so important, we can see we can be something else that transcends the human experience. It is as though once we give up the restrictions that make us human, then The All automatically has a different awareness of itself – we, as a part of The All, perceive it in a greater and more complete sense.

Our fears and desires also restrict our sense of time. In our human form, we need to react here and now or within specific time frames, or something kills us or our lack of human needs being met sees us perish. Our being here is tuned to rates of change around us – what we know as time. For instance, I either pull my foot quickly from the broken glass or I can lose my foot. I either find water within a week or I die of thirst. But when there are no fears to react to and no desires to satisfy, there is no need for time, and I noticed our perception of time completely changes. It is as if we transcend it, but also can notice realms running at different times and expressions of The All beyond the physical. As I became privy to, it seems all the realms are created by altering what I can only describe as restricted fields of change altering time. Even the physical is based on fields of time, giving the illusion of the physical. Like Laozi and others, I cannot put names to all I experienced.

Did I experience God?

If you believe God is in all things and we are God as much as God is us – we are all a manifestation of the same – then yes, I experienced perhaps a truer sense of God than is usually associated with the term.

Then how did our concept of God develop to the point of giving Him the human qualities of vengeance, taking sides in wars, supporting slavery, and threatening us with eternal damnation – a punitive God as Lord and ultimate ruler? How could an eternally peaceful image of balance and harmony be corrupted into a fatherly figure controlling and dominating us, as described in my upbringing? How did loving God come to mean disempowerment and submission – you will do as I say or else?

While in connection with The All, I sensed no desire for war, vengeance, conflict, taking sides or a fight against evil, let alone tyrannical domination. On the contrary, I sensed a subtle harmony without favour or ill intent within what little there was to notice. Some might call what I noticed infinite compassion; to an extent, this is true. Still, once again, the feelings and experiences translate poorly into words. Understand our feelings – as we have come to do – and a potential explanation for how our image of God became altered becomes obvious.

As we have noted, our desire for wealth, power and status corrupts us and drives us towards extremes of imbalance with nature, among each other and within ourselves. Suppose these three malevolent desires drive you. In that case, you are likely to form empires that disregard the peaceful nature of others around us and dominate them – force them into submission. War begets war, and empires beget empires. When writing many of our religious texts, we were regularly at war, part of greater empires or powerful states vying for supremacy and with most of their suffering peoples subjugated to massive inequalities. We do not need an all-powerful, unstoppable, supernatural God or Gods of compassion, friendship, love and peace in such realms. We need an almighty King and leader who is on our side and cares for our well-being, who can empower us with His righteousness, and who favours us above all others. We must be His chosen people.

Why create a vengeful God? One apparent reason is that we keep on the straight and narrow. In a world of brutality driven by fear, fear of the whip or fires of damnation will have more influence than the carrot of kindness, love and caring. A vengeful God also gives us hope and a sense of safety – our human sense for justice or revenge becomes satisfied; they will pay for this and never harm us again.

As we have seen, our desires and fears mould us and determine the expression of our humanity. These desires and fears determine what we notice and how we interpret them – they give everything meaning. They also become part of our stories or narratives about ourselves and the world.

In other words, we experience the world with a human bias. If the bias is corrupted, our stories will be corrupted. Soon, we can create stories that promote imbalance and aren't even close to the peace, harmony and balance we can realise.

It is by recognising the vulnerability of our human bias and how easily it can be corrupted, especially once we disconnect from nature, that we begin to see how simple it is to be led down an imbalanced and unnecessarily destructive path. I suggest we bypass the messengers and search for connection with The All ourselves – no more middlemen. That means no more priests, priestesses, prophets or messengers of God and no more preaching or following supposedly wise and spiritually awakened leaders. It means not using texts as our source of inspiration but actively searching for truth within and connecting with a source much more representative of the true nature of The All – God – found in the natural world.

'But God and His prophets offer us hope,' some may respond. 'I need to feel loved by a greater being I can trust to save me from misery. I need to submit to Him and feel the presence of His love.'

Unfortunately, our world is so brutal we are being treated appallingly and suffer immensely. But if we follow and submit to visions of a God that are not even close to the qualities of The All, what are we submitting to? Is it really God or the ideals and corruptions of men?

As we have seen, human beings were made to be tribal; we feel much greater satisfaction when our friendship needs are satisfied, for instance. Were tribes built upon a system of hierarchy or consensus? Consensus. We each had a valuable say, and if we lived in peace, there was no brutal hierarchy. Hierarchies have their place – for instance, they work well when we need quick decisions, such as during war and within some companies. But our human bias includes our need to be considered equal. Making God into a king or Lord works against our peaceful, balanced inner nature.

Our image of God also sets an example. If God is Lord, then it validates that one man can make themselves higher and rule, oppress and use others for their purpose. If God can have individual power, then so can I, and I can use God's will to justify it. God as Lord disempowers us and makes us submissive and ripe to be ruled by the greedy. The power we give God to save us is the same power we give Him to allow us to be dominated, oppressed and suffer untold misery. Is that the image of God we truly wish to follow?

Yes, there should be great love and compassion in the world. We should live our peaceful ideal because we intuitively know it is possible; it lives within our hearts. But as we look at what wonders and peace there could be, it can seem like the world's problems are brought about by great evil working against great good. We are tempted to submit to personifications of good, love and compassion – 'I will give myself to my loving, compassionate saviour.' And yet, this act of submission also disempowers us and leaves us open to being ruled by others who promote self-interest, greed and inequality – ensuring more misery. Accepting the notion of a battle of good versus evil prevents us from exploring the insights into what we do and why – the ultimate, practical reasons why things are as they are. Submitting to the good or the light keeps us ignorant and ripe for manipulation. Seeking refuge in the so-called good doesn't become a source of salvation but a barrier to realising it.

Could I reconcile the image of God of my childhood with my connection with The All I experienced in my mid-twenties?

I could. And I could also reconcile my experience of The All and the distortive effects of corruptive human bias with every other religious and philosophical belief I had ever considered – a bias that becomes more apparent as we understand our feelings better.

CHAPTER 13

COULD UNDERSTANDING FEELINGS BE OUR GREAT FUTURE HOPE?

The old car would regularly bump across every corrugation or deep road blemish as we passed the majestic ancient eucalypts nestled close to the narrow dirt track weaving its way into seemingly endless bushland. When I was a child, people introduced the country to me as a resource. From as far back as I can recall, the land wasn't seen by those around me as a spiritual place of great wonder but as something we travel through and clear to grow crops and feed livestock. Yes, I found great solace in being alone in nature and absorbing its calming wonder. However, it was still emphasised to me country is something we use. I know indigenous cultures all have their way of describing and relating to the country that embraces them that differs greatly from the views I learned. It is the same natural world, yet we see it differently. Our past lays the foundations for how we interpret our world. In recognising the definitive influences of our past, I realise that every person who experiences and realises The All will apply their experience and the insights it offers differently.

It was no surprise to learn that Laozi's connection with a shamanistic world of a culture deeply rooted in an intimate connection with the natural world would significantly impact his descriptions and teachings. Over time, he gave his wisdom and insights a more nature-focused flavour. The fact the person experiencing transcendence has already lived a life is bound to affect how they then try to interpret and apply their insight. So, too, the influence of those around them in their daily life will affect what they may say, write or try to describe. As we grow, we can often refine and develop our preferred approaches. The books I have written reflect this, the ideas influenced by my past evolving with new experiences and events around me. I have finally come full circle.

Only recently, after writing my book on taming fear, did I begin to appreciate the value and potential of knowing and exploring feelings to help us restore balance within and in the world. I have returned to recalling and more fully integrating the experience of realising The All many decades ago.

Why do I now believe that understanding feelings is our best hope for restoring balance and harmony, and increasing the quality and satisfaction of the human experience? Several reasons.

Firstly, the personal understanding and mastering of feelings empowers us to understand the human experience to the point of being able to master restrictive, traumatic fears and emotional pain. It gives us a practical way to find personal contentment within. We become the masters of how we feel, no longer victims.

Secondly, as we master feelings, we enhance our sense of self and begin to realise the extraordinary potential of the experience of being a human being. We can embrace the desires and pleasures of life rather than see them as the source of our misery. We can revel in being human and help others around us and those who come after us to enjoy the human experience too, always mindful of the need for functional balance.

There is a temptation, if we make realising The All our main focus, that we live a life devoid of pleasure to get there. Should we wish to let our ego die, the process shouldn't last a lifetime, or we become disconnected, dysfunctional, human beings – we set a bad example and perpetuate an imbalance within us and with nature. When we are ready to connect with The All, it should take no more than months, perhaps less. If it takes longer, it is probably worth better preparing ourselves for a later attempt.

Thirdly, with an understanding of feelings as our guide, we are less likely to tolerate hierarchies, being dominated and oppressed. We will no longer aspire to be the rich and powerful; we will recognise their illness and seek a cure. We may someday put our desire for friendship ahead of desire for wealth, power and status.

Fourthly, connecting with and mastering feelings allows us to communicate with representations of nature within us – our more authentic human self, less corrupted – but also to be more open to learning the language of land/country. As Armstrong rightly suggests, as we reconnect emotionally with nature, we will be much better positioned to re-establish a sustainable balance with it. We will again recognise that to harm and disrespect nature is to harm and disrespect ourselves.

Fifth, to better understand feelings is to better understand our bias. We do not see existence as it is, but according to the lens of the feelings that define us – our view of everything is distorted. When we master feelings, we open our minds to a universe of possibilities we never imagined.

If you are sceptical of my experience of The All that is okay; the level of awareness sounds too expansive to be real. But whether you believe in this level of awareness or not, we can still agree that once we reduce our fears and worries about what might be, we can begin to see the physical world in many ways our colleagues may not and be open to whole new fields of study. Imagine what discoveries we can make when we are no longer held back by dogma driven by people's need to feel important.

Sixth, and finally, to understand feelings truly and comprehensively is to automatically begin to realise the impermanence and artificial nature of the ego, all while exploring and living a functional human experience. When we recognise the ego is not much more than the vehicle for our human existence, we don't only empower ourselves, we transform ourselves into a more functional form. We also open ourselves to more easily be prepared to discard ego and experience beyond it.

In other words, once our understanding and wisdom have been enhanced enough by truly knowing and mastering feelings, we are but a short step to realising The All should we choose to. We may realise The All as a natural side effect without significant extra effort once our wisdom is sufficient. Remember, The All can be regarded as the ultimate truth in many ways. Our understanding of feelings is founded upon continuing to search for truth within. Our method of searching for truth within aligns with our destination well – search for truth long enough with an open heart, and we can find a much greater truth, such as The All.

Where does science fit into all this?

As previously alluded to, science is a handy tool, provided it is practised well with sound studies that are reproduced. Science can offer beneficial insight. However, science comes with an inherent flaw that can have devastating consequences. Science needs to realise a bigger picture.

Science, as you are aware relies on and is grounded heavily in logic – properties dominated by our left brain. However, the left brain isn't very good at the big picture and context. That is where our right brain is better; it deals less with specifics and more with how it all fits together – how it feels. Without a right brain to guide it, science can be like running with blinkers on and we are only able to see what is directly in front of our faces. It can be too late by the time we see where we are going and the dangers ahead. When we understand feelings, we engage our right brain. The wisdom and insights gained from engaging our right brain give the benefit of understanding the relevance of what we are doing – it gives science context.

Wisdom built upon an understanding of feelings offers us guidance so we can better put the skills of science to use in a way that creates less damage and imbalance. For instance, we are much less likely to develop weapons that can eliminate all life on earth if we remain in connection with our feelings and the bigger picture, such as nature and The All. We are also less likely to pollute and ravage the natural world by creating chemicals and substances that we know are severely toxic.

How do we reconcile science's search for the ultimate truth vs. our search for personal truth within? After all, the two may clash – what we discover may be at odds with what science discovers.

Like any tool of understanding, science is based on creating stories – in science, we call them theories. But as we learned early, no theory is ultimately correct. That means we don't let science be the gospel; we keep an open mind, and if we have the skill and education, we critically examine the evidence ourselves. However, there are times when the information is so specialised, making sense of it can be challenging. If the stakes are high, such as the results may impact our health, deferring to expert opinion can be practical and prudent. For instance, it may be better to seek a doctor's opinion than to diagnose an illness and decide on treatments for ourselves. First, however, we should find an authority that isn't primarily self-interest driven.

But science is based on fact; surely facts have more weight than our opinions.

We can debate fact – what is and isn't a fact – forever and ultimately get nowhere; even the most robust fact is still an interpretation founded in human bias. So I prefer to focus on functionality rather than facts to bypass this endless arguing.

In other words, let us not ask whether it is a fact; instead, is the theory and the information we are searching for – so-called facts – functional? In short, does the idea work and is the data helpful and usable? Does the information we are acquiring help enhance balance and harmony and give us long-term satisfaction as human beings or not?

For example, is the information obtained by physics from billion-dollar atom smashers useful? Well, so far, nothing useful and practical has come from them. Does smashing atoms help us enhance balance and harmony within ourselves and the world? No. So what is the point in creating so many theories and arguing about how to interpret irrelevant information known by science as facts about subatomic physics? There isn't any, not on a functional level.

A similar example is cosmology: trying to better understand the cosmos by creating more accurate simulations from data gathered about the universe. Is the data about the stars practically useful for us as ordinary human beings? Not really; most of it is useless to you and me. Will the data and understanding of cosmology – the theories and data combined – help us live in greater harmony and balance? Again, no. So why spend billions trying to understand and gather data and then argue about it when it isn't functional?

When we focus our arguments away from what is or isn't fact and what theory is ultimately right or wrong and divert it to asking if it is functional, we refocus our interpretation and the direction of our discoveries. We begin to look at the practical relevance of everything. We must then reconsider what is functional and what balance and harmony mean. At some point, we will need to realise the commonality of all human beings – our basic desires and fears are common to us all and are influenced and determined by nature. Over time, we may even agree on these needs and then work to satisfy them for everyone better – since what we do to one, we do to us all. In a short time with a functional focus, perhaps we may see how toxic greed is, for instance, no matter what 'facts' we choose to look at to try to justify it.

Should we never consider the wonders of the cosmos? On the contrary, I find what happens in the universe interesting. But these details will be more relevant, engaging, and accurate once we visit them personally by traveling among the stars some day – perhaps soon. Until then, isn't it better we focus more on function? At least that way, once we have the technology, we are less likely to sow seeds of imbalance and disharmony wherever we go.

What about indigenous cultures? Where do their beliefs fall in all this?

By their nature, tribal cultures still intimately in contact with nature will be governed by their right brain more than their left – more mythos and less logos. They won't be interested in arguing over facts. Instead, their focus will be on how to get their society and relationships to work and live sustainably with nature around them – their focus will be function. Their stories will, by necessity, be filled with practical narratives reflecting function handed down and refined over generations. Who cares if a spirit is real so long as sharing the story of the spirit helps us get along and live in greater harmony with nature?

To the Western minds focused on logic and fact, the stories of indigenous cultures can seem primitive and just plain wrong. But that is the interpretation of the left-brain-dominated mind. To the right brain, able to see and feel beyond the detail, the indigenous stories are gold, full of wisdom realised over millennia. How sad it is so many indigenous stories and cultural traditions – wisdom – have been lost due to the arrogance of Western thought. Not only were the indigenous peoples able to learn the language of their land, they often had the equivalent of a shaman who had taken inner journeys similar to mine and could share their bigger picture knowledge of the beyond.

Indigenous stories often have greater legitimacy and functional insights than the scientific stories of civilised Western lands. After all, indigenous stories were often far better at helping us satisfy the desires within the BOS Model than we of the modern Western world have been able to achieve.

Until we truly understand the validity of ancient indigenous cultural wisdom, we will be unlikely to respect and accept indigenous people as equals in our societies. I sadly still hear people saying the indigenous are just an inferior, primitive form of man. Understanding feelings may ensure we change that nonsensical view.

How can the language of feelings bring us closer to The All?

We have often alluded to the language of feelings, but what is it? And how can learning this language help us connect closer to The All and be guided by it?

The language of feelings is like the language of the Land/Country we described earlier, giving meaning to what we notice. In the case of feelings, it is recognising the connection between feelings and the underlying scenarios they represent. For example, the scenario that we might lose a job we need right now can evoke feelings of fear. The scenario of first meeting our partner, courting them, building a close, trusted bond and raising a family can incite feelings of joy, love, contentment and physical pleasure. To delve into a feeling and to understand it is to delve into scenarios, how one thing led to another and led to another again, and what these changes mean for us.

Once I could delve into feelings, I found I had a new tool to discover more about the human condition, the nature of the universe and beyond than I could learn within the restrictive confines of being human. Because I had experienced The All, I could better recognise my bias and see some of what is beyond its distortions. I have only now realised and explored some of the feelings I can trace before I was born. I have begun to perceive and access feelings related to before conception, as strange as that might sound, although I don't feel a need to focus on them at this point.

How does knowing the language of feelings bring us closer to The All?

The language of feelings allows us to bypass the inherent bias of words and language. Every word and language reflects our culture and how we interpret the world as a group. As we have seen, our cultures can become very dysfunctional and interpret the world and universe in unhelpful ways. Learning the language of feelings allows us to connect with The All more directly and personally. To tune into our hearts is to connect more directly to the depths of our nature and the balance inherent in The All. It gives us a more direct way of communicating with The All in a purer sense.

Learning the language of feelings is like any skill; it takes practice. We start, and step by step, we progress. Through curiosity, we delve into feelings and ask them questions so they can reveal their nature. Soon, we begin to see how our fears and desires are but a reflection of possible scenarios of losses, gains and hopes that continually govern our thoughts, dreams and actions. We begin to see why we feel the pain of loneliness. We realise how being emotionally neglected affects how we feel now and why our joys are precious, too. Finally, we get to the heart of being human and learn to realise what brings us lasting satisfaction. We know and embody wisdom.

Have I learned all I can from feelings?

Absolutely not. As I mentioned, the more you learn, the more you realise how much you don't know. Understanding feelings offers us ways not just to explore our hearts; it provides insights into the physical world, too.

But what if understanding feelings can also help us access realms beyond the physical? What if being able to notice, use and understand feelings could give us another means to explore the universe and realms that exist beyond time? Had I not experienced The All, I would not have considered these possibilities remotely achievable. Then, I was reminded of parts of the experience of The All that I had forgotten that offered a new and expansive promising hope.

CHAPTER 14

FEELINGS, HOPE AND BEYOND

The desk is wood with a green leather inlay, small, with one set of draws to the right – over twenty years old, a going-away present from the practice I left in Sydney. Dust dulls areas of green, appearing like I haven't cleaned them in years – I have, but dust is relentless. To the right, a closed laptop, cables emerging to external hard drives, speakers and a twenty-seven-inch computer screen. To my left, some mouth mints prevent me from using snacks for added stimulation. As I finalise this book, the question arises, why write it now? And why share my experience realising The All?

Interestingly, I thought about writing a book about the language of feelings over ten years ago. However, the timing wasn't right, and I didn't think people would be interested. Who wants to know about feelings in such a logical world? Instead, I wrote the other books as I believed they might have greater practical value now or in the future. Finally, I realised that perhaps people have less awareness and understanding of their feelings than I assumed. Books talking about human desires? Who would want to know about – let alone want to understand – that? Except for clients and those attending my talks, the topics were not a recognised or popular format. I wrote them anyway. A deeper part of me implored me to write them – so I did.

As I began writing this book, I thought about writing only about feelings. Then, a good quarter into writing it, I realised it lacked critical elements such as the bigger picture – seeing the great potential for insight and transformation in feelings. Even if we understood our feelings well and they began to make sense, giving meaning, purpose and direction in our lives; even if they offered us a way to see past our restrictive fears and unnecessary pains, they lacked a greater sense of direction – where we were going with this and an ultimate goal. Then I realised I had forgotten what I was doing all this for – I had been so caught up in the process I had forgotten a deeper part of myself.

It was as though I was lost in the Matrix and forgot what was on the other side.

But, as has happened many times, the inner, deeper feelings still guided me, whether I was consciously aware of them or not. Yes, I was going about my life as a doctor, treating mental illness and trying to refine ways to help others get better. Still, I had lost sight of my reason for accepting this life and learning all the aspects of living it and the more profound qualities of our mind – until the last six to twelve months before beginning to write this book.

Perhaps it was time to offer further attention back to The All.

I was reluctant to write a book about The All and my experiences, knowing how so many people's ideas on the subject in the past had grown to mythical yet unrealistic and often impractical levels. However, a new level of insight into feelings, developed over the years in writing my past works and sharing them with clients, created a receptive mind for me to understand The All in more straightforward, valuable ways. So maybe The All should be written about.

To help ensure I am not regarded as supernatural – or connected with the supernatural – in any way, I have written about my past and what led me to realise The All. Every step leading up to its realisation was crucial to my being able to see it: being an immigrant from a country once considered the enemy, my parents' and sister's traits and qualities, how others treated me at school and the humiliation by a girl – all were essential. So too, me relating to stories from a guy who had tapped into spiritual and occult beliefs I doubt he understood – the tales of Lobsang Rampa. I was destined to be a doctor. It was preordained I would have a life-threatening crisis that would lead me to consider the only way out was to push my mind and then, without expectation, find answers and contentment in a part of our greater selves – everything and beyond – The All.

The other benefit I wanted to reflect on in sharing some of my early stories was how events affect feelings. Then feelings affect our choices and directions. The insights we have now developed from the beginning to understand the BOS Model, for instance, in hindsight, indicate why I felt so sad and had recurring thoughts of wanting not to be here anymore. How would you feel if your desires and hopes seemed forever quashed to the point you felt destined to only be here for everyone else and never yourself? And yet, how much of the priorities and greed that have permeated the world played a massive role in my melancholy? We live in first-world countries, with more than we need – the envy of over ninety percent of the world – and yet we have made ourselves so miserable. How tragic. How correctable.

I share the events after realising The All in the hope of, once again, reminding us that the process of understanding, realisation and self-transformation takes time and implementing practical steps to make it reality. In a way, there is some truth to the adage that what doesn't kill us makes us stronger. As mentioned, our most incredible insights and transformations often come from the dark. For instance, were it not for my poor and, at times, horrendous experiences with relationships, the BOS Model would not have come to pass. Neither would I have written *The Fall and Rise of Women* or *The Friendship Key* and recognised our inner uncontrolled malevolence and its source. Each book is an insight into our heart's desires and a study of feelings.

As a result of writing these books, do I believe I have all the answers? Quite the opposite.

Everything I have written is just one point of view. The insights within the books allow you to consider your views differently so you may benefit from them. As mentioned, all ideas are a work in progress.

Was Karen Armstrong's book, *Sacred Nature*, the only book that drew me to write about The All? There was another author who helped convince me – John E. Mack.

For those unfamiliar with Mack's work, he was a Pulitzer Prize-winning author and professor of psychiatry at Harvard University before his tragic death in 2009, when he was hit by a car whose driver was inebriated. As a psychiatrist specialising in trauma, he was reluctantly drawn to help people who had described being abducted. Dismissing whether UFOs and aliens exist – he remained a sceptic – what was particularly fascinating was how these experiences had transformed these people's view of themselves and everything. As a result, they began to change his world view too.

Growing up like me with a robust physically focused view of reality and existence founded in measurable and logical science, he began to consider the possibility of realms beyond those of matter.

Being a psychiatrist, he could quickly weed out those suffering from mental illnesses such as psychosis or schizophrenia. And yet, there still seemed to be a shared experience across hundreds of cases – perhaps thousands. The stories were compelling.

I found the stories interesting too. Accounting for each person's bias and interpretations, and setting aside the technologies described, such as time and almost instant travel across the universe, rapid changes of direction that defied known physics, unlimited energy sources and being able to traverse through matter – all of these were unsurprising and consistent with the theories I was privy to soon after connecting with The All. What fascinated me the most was Mack's interpretation of the abductee's own transcendent experiences.

As a specialist in trauma, Mack found the most traumatic part of the abduction experience wasn't being taken apparently against their will and poked and prodded – later, for the most part, they would learn they agreed to it. Instead, the most significant distress came from the assault on their worldview – nothing they had learned about the world and universe was true. If their abductions were real, everything they believed had been turned upside down. Many visitations – abductees would often prefer the term visitations to abductions – described people connecting with these beings in a way they could perceive past themselves, across past lives, and into the universe and beyond.

Whether we believe in UFOs and alien abductions or not, it became fascinating to learn that perhaps there was more than one way to experience a transcendent universal experience. All along, I had believed there was only one way – meditation, though, as mentioned, I didn't consider what I did was meditating at the time. Mack describes three types of experiences that lead to transcendence. I'm paraphrasing since there is no agreed-upon terminology to describe it.

Firstly, a near-death experience. A significant number of people who return from apparent death describe an experience of perceiving the greater whole that transcends time. I know of at least one author who has expressed their near-death experience similarly. Another way is through deep meditation, as I did. And another seemed to be through the abduction experiences. None of the abductees had any notions of broader universal awareness before their experiences; for the most part, they lived regular lives.

Connections with The All or a similar experience may be achievable in several ways.

I don't find having to die or experience alien abduction to gain transcendence appealing. But, interestingly, people with no inclination towards experiencing anything similar to connection with The All would have experiences that seemed similar to realising It.

Mack's work was unsurprisingly controversial. He almost lost his tenure after writing his first book on the subject – *Abduction*.

How did Mack's books influence my decision to write about The All? He, like Karen Armstrong, reminded me of how many of us over millennia are drawn to such profound transcendent experiences. He also reminded me how transformative the transcendent experience can be and how it can offer guidance.

Was there anything in Mack's books or the stories of visitations that altered my worldview? No. However, another possibility took some time to integrate – how technology might someday allow us to enter dreams and life before and after death. Would the physics theories I happened upon after realising The All allow for this? Yes, it could. However, it isn't the technology or physics theories I believe we should focus on. Besides, if entering other realms, including beyond death, is achievable, are we ready to integrate it into our lives? Especially while we suffer so much internal imbalance and have such a poor understanding of our feelings.

As I write this book about The All and feelings, I am also aware it can challenge our worldview, hopefully positively. However, unless we are prepared to see beyond our fears and pains, seeing and realising a more expansive way of viewing ourselves, the universe and beyond can be highly challenging. For example, are we prepared to consider the idea we are expressions of multi-temporal beings – living across many times simultaneously – as we live a more restrictive 'physical' life here? Are we open to the possibility that even non-human entities – some living in different realms of time we might call different dimensions – and we are all part of a connected greater whole – part of The All we can all gain guidance from? Could our whole view of our life and the universe be way off the mark?

As you can see, I am open to many possibilities knowing that we will eventually learn what is closer to reality – truth – what works and what doesn't.

Ultimately, I write this book now because I am comfortable knowing it is the right time.

I envision a future that continues uniting us through self-understanding, embracing the commonalities of our human experience, and restoring a balance with nature and within ourselves. There is harmony within our hearts and beyond, waiting to be nurtured and realised. As we have learned, there are simple steps we can each take to make such a world reality.

I feel hope for the future.

What do you feel?

ABOUT THE AUTHOR

Dr. Winfried Sedhoff was born in Germany and immigrated with his parents and older sister to the southern New South Wales country city of Albury, Australia when he was eighteen months of age. He fondly spent many of his early years visiting local farms and helping muster sheep or cattle. The family moved onto a farm thirty minutes drive out of town two years before he completed high school. He graduated in medicine (M.B.B.S.) from New South Wales University in 1987.

Barely two years after graduating and with a promising specialist career before him, he suffered a life-threatening personal crisis and resigned from the training course. Soon, he found himself living in self-imposed isolation and began a quest within himself to find a sense of truth, a genuine sense of self that could relieve him of the depression that had dogged him since his early high school years. Within three months, he found what he was searching for. It was like nothing he expected.

Winfried has been a general practitioner for over thirty years. The last twenty-plus years have been spent specialising in mental health and applying some of what he learned during his internal quest. He now lives in Brisbane, Australia.

ACKNOWLEDGEMENTS

To my dear family, friends, and the many people who have played a crucial role in shaping my life, I offer profound thanks. Your influence and support have been instrumental in the creation of this book, and it would not have been possible without all of you.

I want to express my gratitude to Susan Lee and Heather Millar, my editors at different stages of the book, for their guidance and invaluable recommendations. I also extend a big thank you to George Stevens for the brilliant cover design and layout of the book's internals. Our collaboration was not just productive, but a true delight.

My sincere thanks go out to everyone who has been part of my journey, refining my ideas and allowing me to share them over the last decades. Your feedback and support have been instrumental in shaping the content of this book.

www.ingramcontent.com/pod-product-compliance
Lightning Source LLC
Chambersburg PA
CBHW061734070526
44585CB00024B/2665